FIGHT RIGHT

FOR YOUR

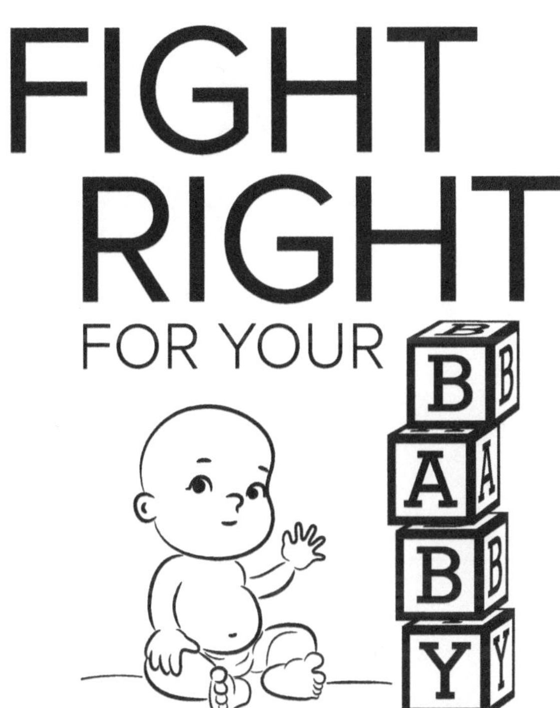

The How-To Guide for Expecting and New Parents to Shift from Conflict to Connection

**Rhona Berens, PhD, PCC and
Tina Stanley, MSW, LCSW**

"A superb book. I highly recommend it. You will gain a lot of insight and information to help you be the parents you always wanted to be. I love this book!"

> – Lynn Lott, mother, international speaker, parenting authority, and co-author of *Chores Without Wars*; *The Family That Works Together*; *Positive Discipline A-Z*; *Positive Discipline for Teenagers*

"As a 30 year veteran in the perinatal/lactation world and someone who has been married for 30 years, I can truly say I wish I had found this book at the beginning of my career *and* my marriage. As brand new parents it would have been a gift to have this treasure trove of activities to work through common challenging issues that most parents experience. It could have acted as a salve on some of the wounds we caused one another because we had so few tools early on in marriage. This book provides those tools. It also offers options for couples to work on together or even on one's own. It provides multiple ways to "fight right," so parents can pick what will work best for them. It is my sincere wish that in addition to purchasing all of the baby gear when couples go through pregnancy, they will also pick up this book!"

> – Laurel Wilson, IBCLC, BSc, RLC, CLE®, CCCE, CLD, CPPI, co-author of *The Attachment Pregnancy*; and *The Greatest Pregnancy Ever*

"*Fight Right for Your Baby* is chock-full of evidence-based information for parents on how to work as a team, foster compassion and enjoy the parenting process together. Berens and Stanley use their combined experience and expertise to help parents neutralize conflict and embrace what matters most in a family: connection, love, and respect. I highly recommend this impactful book."

> – Donna Tetreault, journalist and best-selling, award-winning author of *The C.A.S.T.L.E. Method* and *Dear Me*

"*Fight Right for Your Baby* is a book that all my clients need. It illuminates how we often default to old dysfunctional coping patterns that can be destructive; however, we are capable of making real changes. This book can transform our conflicts from hurtful to hopeful."

> – Gabrielle Kaufman, LPCC, Certified Perinatal Mental
> Health Clinician, and former Clinical Director for
> Maternal Mental Health NOW

"I love this book! I hope that Rhona and Tina come up with their own curriculum to teach effective and heart felt "fighting right" to grade school kids. Meanwhile, I will have to make do with getting this book into the hands of every couple that I work with. *Fight Right for Your Baby*'s guiding principles transcend individual relationships and make a universal call to step into discomfort for the sake of growth. If you are questioning your ability to fight skillfully while being rooted in love and respect, this is the book for you. If you would like to move from disruption to connection, this is the book for you. If you are looking for ways to understand your partner and (equally, if not more importantly) understand *yourself* when the inevitable fights arise, this is the book for you. Rhona and Tina have left you and me, and our children, a great gift within these pages."

> – Kelly Gray, Childbirth Educator, birth worker, and
> author of *Instructions for an Animal Body*; *My Fingers and
> Whales and other stories of Cetology*; *Tiger Paw, Tiger Paw,
> Knife, Knife*

"Rhona and Tina offer a framework of what it takes to have a healthy and fulfilling family life. They provide a set of strategies that are accessible and practical to build the health and wellness of your relationship, your children, and your family system. Thank you, Tina and Rhona, for all your hard work and thoughtfulness."

> – Mark Collin, MA, MFT, author and founder of
> Toolbox Project®

To our families, friends, and clients:
*Thank you for teaching us
the value of learning to Fight Right.*

Table of Contents

Acknowledgments

Writing a book is always a collaborative endeavor and we want to express our gratitude to those who have helped us take *Fight Right for Your Baby* from its inception to birth.

Lynn Lott, Laurel Wilson, Robin Fisher-Tachouet, and Kelly Gray read drafts of this book and offered invaluable insights and suggestions to improve it. Thank you to Paula Gray and Rachel Shipps for drawing illustrations that, while they didn't make it into the final version, provided us with imaginative possibilities that helped us refine the visual style of *Fight Right for Your Baby*. Thank you to Mark A. Collin, Jonathan Foust, Marita Fridjhon and the Center for Right Relationship, and Brent Kessel and Spencer Sherman for letting us share some of their concepts, questions, and tools. Thanks, too, to Shev Rush for his expert advice and assistance with marketing and PR.

We are grateful to our editor, Jennifer Jas, whose guidance and suggestions inspired us to rework and revise sections of this book and add new content, all of which greatly improved *Fight Right for Your Baby*. Our book designer, Carla Green, not only virtually held our hands throughout the editorial and design process, she did an exceptional job listening closely and respectfully to what we envisioned and capably turned our vision into a beautiful book.

Thank you to our families for their loving support and patience as we birthed this book. Last but not least, our heartfelt gratitude to all of the perinatal practitioners, parenting professionals, and expecting and new parents with whom we've worked. Your experiences and wisdom have guided us in writing this book and helped us stay the course to create a resource that we hope eases and reduces the negative impacts of Fighting Wrong, and inspires curiosity, exploration, and growth as future generations of expecting and new parents learn to *Fight Right for Your Baby.*

Introduction

How to Get the Most Out of This Book

We wrote *Fight Right for Your Baby* to make your passage into new parenthood easier and as supportive as possible for your relationship and your baby's developmental health. This book empowers you to take care of your child and your relationship simultaneously by learning how to "do" conflict constructively and how to repair it effectively. *Fight Right for Your Baby* provides expecting couples and new parents—those valiantly trying to avoid prenatal or postpartum conflict *and* those in the thick of it—with quick and easy tools to transform damaging fights into productive disagreements and to help you make up with each other in ways that nourish your relationship and your baby.

> **Babies need—really need—parents who respect each other, collaborate well, and know how to get through conflict constructively.**

Babies need—really need—parents who respect each other, collaborate well, and know how to get through conflict constructively. Parents need that, too, especially because so many are unprepared for the stress that a baby puts on their relationship.

Regardless of how close expecting parents feel before their baby arrives, most new parents report a drop in relationship satisfaction in the first one to three years after the birth of their first child. That drop is steep for two out of three couples, and most cite a significant increase in conflict. If you're experiencing this type of shift in your relationship, the good news is you're not alone. The other good news is this book will help you intervene in this downtrend, increase your relationship satisfaction, and support your baby's* wellbeing.

In this book, you will learn how to:

+ Fight Right to support your baby's developmental health.
+ Avoid and reduce negative relationship conflict.
+ Cultivate a fulfilling relationship, even when you disagree.
+ Understand the impact of parenthood on your relationship satisfaction.
+ Repair the damage and distress caused when you Fight Wrong.
+ Strengthen your relationship.
+ Approach parenthood as a collaborative team.

Differences abound in how people learn and prefer to communicate. Some are kinesthetic learners and enjoy tangible, physical experiences over reading or listening, which are the preferred formats for linguistic and auditory learners. Some are introverts and like to process ideas and experiences internally and nonverbally, while others are extroverts who relish talking and social learning. Some identify as ambiverts and prefer to toggle between inner and outer states. None is better than another, yet negative conflict abounds when you

---

* Although the word "baby" appears in singular form throughout the book, our intent is to be inclusive of multiples, such as twins and triplets.

assume your style is preferable and when you judge your spouse's approach.[†]

While books, by their very nature, offer a more passive learning style, in *Fight Right for Your Baby*, you'll discover adaptable tools. Feel free to add your own kinesthetic "spin" by standing up, walking around, or acting out exercises. In *Fight Right for Your Baby*, we encourage you to use tools in conversation with your partner. Yet, if you're introverted, or if conversations often spark negative conflict, consider sharing written responses with each other before, or instead of, a discussion. If one of you loves talking and the other prefers writing, alternate between those styles, or create a hybrid approach. Bottom line: Make these tools your own.

Together, Rhona Berens, PhD, PCC, and Tina Stanley, MSW, LCSW, have more than forty-five years of experience helping couples and families. The authors know that, with the right kind of support and information, most of you can significantly improve your skills in resolving conflict *and* increase your fulfillment as new parents.

Rhona Berens is a Gottman Educator for *Bringing Baby Home*, a Gottman Leader for *The Seven Principles for Making Marriage Work*, a Certified *Positive Discipline* Parent Educator, and a credentialed coach who helps expecting couples and parents stay sane and stay together. As a mom to two fabulous, complex, and fiery children, Rhona knows firsthand that parenting takes its toll on even the best of relationships, which is why she tries and fails and tries again to walk her talk with her wife and kids. It's also why she offers parents, and the perinatal

---

[†] In *Fight Right for Your Baby*, we primarily use the terms "spouse" and "partner" to refer to your significant other, and at times, we insert "mate" or "beloved" instead. Please feel free to substitute any other term that might better fit your relationship, including making terms plural if you are polyamorous.

and parenting professionals who support them, fun and easy tools for connection and productive communication. This book was born from Rhona's desire to help you better navigate the heightened conflict and dissatisfaction that often accompany new parenthood.

Tina Stanley has been working as a psychotherapist, medical social worker, and hypnotherapist for over thirty years in private practice. She has worked in medical and mental health settings specializing in perinatal mood disorders, parenting issues, and couples therapy. Currently, Tina also specializes in working with clients to support their creative flow and spiritual healing. After repeatedly witnessing the "in the trenches" quality many couples experience as new parents, she has come to believe passionately in the value of proactive preparation and accessible, user-friendly support. Her intention in this book is to help make the passage into parenthood easier for the sake of parents and babies. Tina is also a wife and mother and has learned a great deal, especially humility and a sense of humor, from her own family life.

Please keep in mind: While each relationship is unique, everyone disagrees sometimes. This book is written with diverse relationships and families in mind: expecting and new parents who are married, unmarried, straight, gay, queer, trans, poly, as well as blended, adoptive, and foster families.

Throughout the book, you'll see Quick Questions boxes. We invite you to pause, take a few deep breaths, and ponder the questions and your answers. This practice will help you personalize the information and get the most out of the book, whether you write or talk through your answers, or both.

QUICK QUESTIONS

- What do you hope to get out of this book?
- What attitudes about reading this book, and about your spouse, will best serve your relationship (e.g., curiosity, optimism, compassion, accountability)?
- What would help you be willing to look at your part in unproductive conflict?
- How can you infuse humor or lightness into issues you often take seriously?
- How will you know this book is helping you and your relationship?

PART ONE

Fighting Right

Fighting Right means tackling conflict as a team and adopting a win-win mentality. It means believing—or trying to believe—your partner's opinions, needs, and feelings are as valid as your own.

You won't find a simple formula or rulebook to Fight Right. Yet the tools and suggestions in *Fight Right for Your Baby* depend on a foundation of respect for your partner and a willingness to honestly look at yourself and change your responses both during and after a fight. This foundation is important, so let's expand on those ideas:

- Fighting Right relies on mutual respect.

- Fighting Right depends on taking responsibility for your role in conflict.

- Fighting Right invites you to shift how you disagree and how you make up, so conflict ebbs and flows through your relationship instead of exploding your connection and threatening your family's wellbeing.

- Fighting Right depends on paying attention to process over content: *How* you fight matters more than *what* you fight about.

As you make your way through this book, this foundation will serve you well, as will the Guiding Principles in Chapter 1.

Guiding Principles for
Fight Right for Your Baby

These Guiding Principles inform and support the practical tools in this book. They invite you to reconsider your beliefs about conflict and consciously work to change counter-productive attitudes and behaviors.

1. Conflict is normal and unavoidable.
2. Most people are unskilled at conflict, yet everyone can learn to Fight Right.
3. Conflict can connect you in a positive way.
4. You cannot change your spouse's attitudes and actions.
5. You can change your attitudes and actions.
6. In relationships, everyone is right to some degree.
7. Agreeing with each other is optional, yet trying to understand each other is essential.
8. Friendship and connection are key to relationship satisfaction.
9. You cannot fix your relationship or each other once and for all.
10. There is more than one way to Fight Right.

Since these principles inform so much of this book, they warrant closer consideration.

Guiding Principle #1:
Conflict is normal and unavoidable.

This principle contradicts a dominant cultural assumption: Conflict can and should be avoided. Despite its popularity, that belief ignores lived reality. Disagreement and struggle are natural aspects of human existence. In other words, conflict is normal and to be expected. It's a given that two people sharing daily life, especially with a new baby, will disagree about some things. If you understand and accept that's the case, you begin to normalize your differences and increase your tolerance for *not* being on the same page as your spouse.

Guiding Principle #2:
Most people are unskilled at conflict,
yet everyone can learn to Fight Right.

Unless you studied conflict resolution and now capably model the skills you learned, or you had unusually good role models for productive conflict in your family of origin, you probably know how to Fight Wrong far better than how to Fight Right. Fighting Right is a set of skills and attitudes that you can learn and improve with practice.

Guiding Principle #3:
Conflict can connect you in a positive way.

This principle contrasts with the popular belief that conflict is bad. Yet the act of disagreeing with others is neither inherently good nor bad. It just is. Fighting Wrong can definitely be destructive and precipitate poor outcomes. However, given the right communication skills, conflict can be informative and productive, even beneficial to your relationship. In the best-case scenario, disagreeing in a skillful way nurtures intimacy and connection and deepens mutual understanding and compassion.

Guiding Principle #4:
You cannot change your spouse's attitudes and actions.

The desire to change the people closest to you, especially when you disagree with them, is understandable. While you might make your best efforts to do so, no matter how hard you try, you are doomed to fail: No one has the power to change someone else other than the someone else in question. Grappling with and trying to accept your powerlessness in this regard is an important ingredient in Fighting Right and helps create the foundation for a respectful and satisfying relationship.

Guiding Principle #5:
You can change your attitudes and actions.

This variation on the Serenity Prayer nicely sums up this Guiding Principle: "Grant me the serenity to accept the people I cannot change, the courage to change the one I can, and the wisdom to know it's me." While changing someone else isn't within your grasp, you possess the ability to transform yourself, to shift your attitudes and actions in ways that support positive communication and productive conflict.

Guiding Principle #6:
In relationships, everyone is right to some degree.

Disagreements often happen when you and your partner express contrasting opinions, beliefs, ideas, strategies, values, or feelings. While you might insist your viewpoint is objective because it seems that way to you, it's usually rooted in your own experiences—and not universally accepted facts—so it remains primarily subjective. By shifting away from black-and-white, right-and-wrong dichotomies and accepting that you are often both right to some degree, you intervene in negative conflict and set the stage for Fighting Right. This ties in nicely with Guiding Principle #7.

Guiding Principle #7:
Agreeing with each other is optional, yet trying to understand each other is essential.

Far too often, we confuse the meaning of understanding others versus agreeing with others. Yet the distinctions between understanding and agreeing are noteworthy. Trying to understand someone means you do your best to "get" their perspective, to grasp why they feel, respond, or make choices the way they do, even if you feel, respond, or make choices differently. Curiosity and acceptance of differences are key components of understanding. Because productive conflict depends on respecting differences, letting your spouse know that you understand them enhances Fighting Right. By contrast, agreeing means you are in alignment with each other, and it highlights similarities between you and those with whom you agree. While agreeing with your spouse is nice, it's by no means necessary to Fight Right.

Guiding Principle #8:
Friendship and connection are key to relationship satisfaction.

In committed partnerships, people often focus on and prioritize romance and forget the centrality of friendship. Yet cultivating your friendship and connection with each other provides a foundation for individual and relationship satisfaction *and* supports your ability to Fight Right.

Guiding Principle #9:
You cannot fix your relationship or each other once and for all.

People commonly believe they should aim for a goal or finish line for relationships when everything will be harmonious. This is a variation of the "happily ever after" myth, which privileges perfection and absolutes. Yet relationships are filled with paradox, imperfection, and messiness. They have rhythms. Sometimes situations are harder to deal with; sometimes easier. Sometimes you face big triggers, such as parenthood, job loss, and major illness; sometimes your life together flows smoothly. Sometimes you struggle to connect; sometimes intimacy thrives. No universal goal line exists for individual or relationship wellbeing, only your own best efforts to keep growing.

Guiding Principle #10:
There is more than one way to Fight Right.

The bad news is there's no single proven formula for Fighting Right. The good news is there are multiple paths to handling conflict with skill. You can find the strategies in the pages of this book that work best for you and your relationship.

Although we use the phrases "Fight Right" and "Fight Wrong" for simplicity's sake, other descriptors for this distinction between conflict styles include helpful-unhelpful, productive-unproductive, and skillful-unskillful.

QUICK QUESTIONS

- What does Fighting Right mean to you?
- Which Guiding Principles grab your attention the most?
- In your relationship, which Guiding Principles challenge you the most?
- What might be possible if your disagreements became opportunities to understand each other better, find creative solutions, and solidify your partnership?

CHAPTER 2

What Are the Rewards of Fighting Right?

When you Fight Right, you powerfully support your children's wellbeing, even during infancy. Babies and older kids, too, are sponges. They absorb joy, respect, and friendship; they also absorb tension, resentment, stress, and hostility.

When we encourage you to Fight Right, we mean doing a good enough job, not a perfect one. When you do a good enough job of Fighting Right, you support your baby's successful accomplishment of the first foundational and essential developmental task: establishing a sense of safety and trust in the world. That secure foundation forms the basis for tackling *all* other challenges ahead.

We cannot overstate the importance of this concept: Your baby needs a safe, consistent, and secure relationship with you while transitioning into the external world and slowly developing a sense of self, competence, and mastery. Your positive, supportive relationship with your partner contributes in important ways to that safety.

> *Your baby needs a safe, consistent, and secure relationship with you while transitioning into the external world.*

In our work with parents, we've noticed these rewards of Fighting Right:

+ Improved behaviors and overall wellbeing in children.
+ Heightened individual fulfillment and self-regulation.
+ Increased teamwork, friendship, and intimacy.
+ Enhanced mutual respect.
+ Decreased stress and better sleep.
+ Improved conflict resolution.
+ Enhanced and effective relationship repair.
+ Diminished intensity and frequency of negative conflicts.
+ Bolstered individual and relationship resiliency.
+ Increased openness to bigger-picture thinking.

Fighting Right also increases a sense of safety and enjoyment in your relationship. When you disagree productively, you feel more understood and respected, connected, and open to intimacy. You build trust in each other and in your ability to have honest, healthy disagreements without damaging your relationship and, more importantly, while deepening your bond.

PART TWO

Fighting Wrong

Fighting Wrong means facing off against each other as adversaries and adopting a win-lose mentality. It refers to counterproductive styles of conflict that get in the way of addressing and working through whatever topic or issue caused the disagreement. It breeds tension, misunderstanding, and resentment, and it blocks teamwork.

In this section, we offer insights into Fighting Wrong, the primary way in which many people handle conflict. In an effort to deepen your understanding of the stakes involved in how you navigate conflict, we explore how Fighting Wrong damages your relationship fulfillment and your children's health.

CHAPTER 3

How Does Fighting Wrong Become a Habit?

We learn a lot from those around us while we are growing up—teachers, family, peers, community—yet we rarely learn the skills to Fight Right. Instead, we absorb the finer points of Fighting Wrong from our families and society, including TV shows, movies, and online media, which rely on dramatic, destructive conflict to keep us watching.

Sometimes we Fight Wrong because of our baggage: old hurts, grievances, or traumas. Even when we know better, even when we try to avoid harsh ways of communicating, we get triggered and act out or back away. We feel hurt, angry, scared, or numb and our autonomic nervous system goes on alert. Fight, flight, or freeze impulses kick in, and we lash out, retreat, or feel paralyzed. When that happens, we literally cannot access the more competent, grounded, and mature parts of our brain—the ones that help us empathize, collaborate, negotiate, achieve goals, and just simply think clearly.

> *We absorb the finer points of Fighting Wrong from our families and society.*

Another common reactive behavior that contributes to Fighting Wrong is fawning, also known as people-pleasing or appeasing. What connects fawning to Fighting Wrong? If you prioritize pleasing or placating your spouse over speaking your truth, you often engage in conflict avoidance and allow resentment to build beneath the surface of your relationship. Left untended, unexpressed feelings and opinions eventually erupt in criticism or defensiveness, manifest as withdrawal, morph into negative perceptions of your partner, or generate hopelessness about yourself or your relationship.

The unproductive conflict style (or styles) you witnessed and used while you were growing up often becomes habitual over time, part of a well-worn neural pathway in your brain and nervous system. You Fight Wrong, then, because it's familiar, because it's the norm in North American culture, and because it might have served a protective purpose when you were young. For example, you might have learned to criticize when you tried to hold your own with a bossy older sibling or you learned to avoid conflict as a way to prevent a parent from lashing out verbally or physically.

Because everyone brings patterns and beliefs from the past into relationships and parenting in the present, becoming more conscious and intentional about conflict helps us unlearn Fighting Wrong and create our own version of Fighting Right.

CHAPTER 4

How Does Fighting Wrong Impact Babies and Children?

When your competent, centered, adult self goes underground and Fighting Wrong prevails, you threaten your fulfillment, parenting effectiveness, and children's developmental health. Research indicates that the quality of parents' relationships—which is often tied to parents' conflict styles—is crucial to the wellbeing of kids of all ages, including babies. Studies also show a link between parents' relationship problems and babies' sleep challenges, and recent research suggests a connection between parental conflict and infants' brain and sensory functioning.

Kids who grow up in high-conflict families are more likely than their peers to struggle.

Kids who grow up in high-conflict families are more likely than their peers to struggle with academic achievement and social, problem-solving, and interpersonal skills. They tend to have more conflict with parents, siblings, and peers, and they exhibit more health challenges.

Here are examples of the types of parental conflict that negatively affect babies and children:

- Physically threatening, aggressive, or violent behavior.

+ Frequent fights about the kids or parenting-related topics, such as bedsharing, childcare, and sleep training.
+ Frequent unskilled conflict within earshot of the baby, including a sleeping baby.
+ Verbal or emotional hostility, e.g., biting sarcasm, name-calling, and gaslighting.
+ Withdrawal behaviors, such as when one partner leaves during a fight or refuses to discuss an issue.
+ Frequent heated or intense disagreements.
+ Nonverbal hostile behavior, e.g., "the silent treatment," eye-rolling, and door slamming.
+ Fights that a spouse or the children believe threaten family stability.
+ Festering fights that rarely achieve repair, resolution, or conclusion.
+ Disagreements that leave the baby (or older child) visibly upset.
+ Fights that disrupt the baby's (or older children's) sleep patterns.

Recognize yourself or your relationship on this list? If so, you're not alone. Many parents commonly Fight Wrong. That's why we wrote this book: to teach you how to Fight Right and reduce the destructive impact when you Fight Wrong.

Important variables influence the severity of the negative outcomes of Fighting Wrong. They include:

+ The intensity and tone of your fights.
+ The frequency of your conflicts.
+ Your behaviors toward each other during and after disagreements.

+ What you fight about.
+ Whether or not you resolve or repair conflicts.
+ How you repair after conflicts.

If your fights sometimes get physical or verbally or emotionally abusive, we recommend that you and your spouse obtain immediate professional support from a therapist. Also, please get help individually, especially if your spouse is unwilling to do so.[1]

As daunting as all this sounds, how you Fight Wrong offers clues and strategies to help you learn to Fight Right. Still not clear on Fighting Wrong? Understanding the four most common toxic communication styles helps, and you'll find them in Chapter 5.

> **How you Fight Wrong offers clues and strategies to help you learn to Fight Right.**

Common Ways to Fight Wrong

According to research conducted in the United States by Dr. John Gottman, most people are skilled in at least one of these four common negative conflict styles, and some master more than one:

+ **Contempt/Disrespect**: Condescending or degrading communication that appears in what you say *or* how you say things, e.g., biting sarcasm and eye-rolling. Some people disguise contempt (or criticism) by claiming humorous intent, such as, "I was *joking!*" or deflecting responsibility, as in, "You're so sensitive!" In marriages, contempt is the number one predictor of divorce.

+ **Blame/Criticism**: Attacking, critiquing, or nagging—meaning, making things personal—as opposed to gently complaining or neutrally referencing a challenging issue or behavior. Criticism and blame can also be expressed nonverbally with judgmental grunts or exasperated sighs.[2]

+ **Defensiveness**: Resisting accountability for your role in creating or contributing to negative conflicts, sometimes by resorting to excuses and sometimes

> by reflexively counterattacking. The phrase "having a chip on your shoulder" applies and shows up in what one says, including "It's not my fault!"—and in the person's posture, including crossed arms and "Don't look at me" shrugs.

+ **Stonewalling/Silent Treatment/Avoidance**: Walking away from conflict or remaining physically present yet refusing to engage around or discuss the topic. This unproductive style rests on an unwillingness to productively address a contentious issue and manifests as literal or figurative withdrawal.

Let's differentiate stonewalling—a conflict style in which the decision of whether to engage in conversation remains somewhat within your control—from flooding, which is a physiological response to stress, trauma, or conflict. Here, you are literally flooded with stress hormones, an accelerated heart rate, sweaty palms, or other physiological responses. While flooding makes it hard for some people to back off from Fighting Wrong because their autonomic nervous systems are so revved up, for others flooding shuts down the ability to speak or engage, so it looks a lot like stonewalling.

While stonewalling and flooding sometimes present similarly, when a person stonewalls, they have a greater ability in the moment to change or limit the impact of their conflict style. By contrast, someone who floods needs time to physiologically calm down and self-soothe. This is true regardless of what conflict style we engage in. Whether we start out criticizing, stonewalling, or being contemptuous or defensive, flooding overwhelms us and shuts down the possibility of shifting into productive communication.

If you or your spouse flood during conflict, allow a minimum of twenty minutes to calm down before broaching the topic again. Some people need longer to self-regulate.[*]

Recognizing your go-to toxic communication style enhances your awareness of *how* you approach and express conflict with your beloved *and* how you Fight Wrong. When you activate one of the four styles—e.g., you broach a topic by criticizing your partner or get defensive when they raise an issue with you—the *way* you communicate overrides *what* you say. In other words, style wins out over content. Most disagreements remain unresolved if you, your spouse, or both of you lapse into any of these toxic communication styles and refuse to repair the relationship after the dust settles.

---

[*] See Tool 29, Deal with Flooding, and Tool 30, Practice Self-Soothing.

CHAPTER 6

Transforming Fighting Wrong to Fighting Right

We noted earlier that understanding how you Fight Wrong can help you learn to Fight Right. One way to do so is by inverting contempt, criticism, defensiveness, and stonewalling into opposite behaviors. Since contempt centers on disrespect and condescension, try to prioritize respect, equality, and equity. Similarly, turn criticism and blame into appreciation and discernment, shift from defensiveness to accountability, or morph stonewalling and shutting down into engagement and openness.*

> **Refocus from where or when you disagree to how you disagree.**

Another way to transform Fighting Wrong into Fighting Right is to refocus from where or when you disagree to how you disagree. Some parents take pride in squabbling behind closed doors or delaying conflict until after the baby is asleep. Yet if you still Fight Wrong in those circumstances, how you disagree remains impactful. From infancy onward, kids possess a keen awareness of their parents' moods, energy, and

---

* For exercises to support these shifts, see Tool 7, Acknowledgments and Appreciations, and Tool 9, What's Important to You about That?

feelings. That awareness penetrates walls and slumber. Also, as long as you keep verbal, emotional, or physical abuse at bay, and contempt to a minimum, Fighting Wrong occasionally gives you an opportunity to model repairing with each other in their presence. This is a life skill central to relationship connection and satisfaction. Finally, Fighting Right when children of any age are present normalizes disagreement and teaches them how to address differences respectfully.

We want to emphasize that feeling and expressing anger do not necessarily mean you are Fighting Wrong. Certainly, Fighting Wrong can—and often does—include anger at your spouse, yet not all expressions of anger are inherently negative or destructive. You may tend to resist or suppress your anger—maybe because you believe you don't have a right to it, you worry it will cause damage to your relationships, you've been told to bury or hide it, or you fear that if you start letting it out, you won't stop. However, permitting yourself to feel and express anger will potentially bring you closer to your spouse. Anger, like all other emotions, can serve a purpose. It can energize, motivate, and assist you with setting boundaries. Expressing your anger without blame or criticism can help your partner understand what's important to you. The skilled expression of anger can, then, be part of Fighting Right.

QUICK QUESTIONS

- How was conflict handled in your family growing up?
- What do you like about how it was handled?
- What do you dislike about how it was handled?
- What approaches to conflict, if any, do you want to carry forward from your childhood and use when communicating with your spouse about challenging topics?
- Of the four most prevalent toxic communication styles—contempt, criticism, defensiveness, and stonewalling—which one (or more than one) is your go-to style for negative conflict?
- If your style isn't among those four, how would you describe the way you Fight Wrong?

CHAPTER 7

Why Do You Fight Wrong Even When You Know Better?

Sometimes you Fight Wrong because pointing out how your mate is failing, or insisting that you're right, just plain feels better—in the short run, *a lot* better—than admitting you're not sure how to do things or remaining open to the possibility that there's more than one way to parent.

It's very human to want to win. Our brains support that impulse by grouping experiences as win-or-lose, right-or-wrong dichotomies. Yet if we make a conscious decision to reach for a bigger perspective that serves our individual needs and the needs of our relationship and family, then we invite win-win possibilities. Doing so is important because when you Fight Wrong, you won't find any long-term payoffs for you, your relationship, or your baby.

When you Fight Wrong, you won't find any long-term payoffs for you, your relationship, or your baby.

Fleeting short-term payoffs, however, can keep parents digging in their heels around unproductive conflict and can sometimes feel really satisfying, even as you remain stuck in familiar, unproductive, and even painful patterns.

Short-term payoffs include:

+ Feeling right and righteous.
+ Avoiding a debate.
+ Winning an imaginary competition for the most put-upon, tired, or hard-working parent—what one client dubs "The Suffering Olympics."
+ Bypassing the effort to learn a new mindset or behavior.
+ Sidestepping responsibility for your part in a disagreement.

Another underlying cause of Fighting Wrong, even when you have an intellectual understanding of how to Fight Right, relates to your and your partner's attachment styles. According to attachment theory, our earliest relationships with caregivers significantly influence how we form connections and maintain relationships throughout life. Additional factors that exert an influence on attachment styles include trauma, discrimination, poverty, and other significant disruptions to safety.

Generally speaking, if your caregivers were mostly stable, consistent, and responsive, you likely developed a secure attachment style, meaning, you are usually able to form and maintain stable, close, trusting bonds with others and to capably navigate and repair disruptions to those bonds. Another characteristic of secure attachment is the ability to tolerate emotional discomfort during periods of relationship distress or disconnection.

Three types of insecure attachment can result when early needs for stability and security were not adequately met: anxious, avoidant, or disorganized. An anxious style is characterized by an insistent desire for closeness, a sensitivity to rejection, and a tendency to seek or want frequent reassurance. An avoidant style includes a strong desire for space and independence, and an aversion to emotional expression and intimacy. The disorganized style is uncommon and tends to result from severe trauma. This style is what it sounds like: a confused alternation between wanting closeness and distance.

Whether you possess the same attachment style as your partner, attachment styles influence how smoothly you dance together when conflict arises, how frequently you step on each other's toes, or how often you leave your partner alone on the dance floor.

The most common attachment-related dances are:

+ You both approach conflict calmly and productively: secure with secure.
+ You both resist addressing and resolving conflict: avoidant with avoidant.
+ You both bring a lot of emotional intensity to conflict with an urgent need to resolve it, often in unskilled ways: anxious with anxious.
+ One of you is reluctant to address conflict, while the other insists on doing so: avoidant with anxious.

These styles are not carved in stone. Someone with avoidant tendencies likely also grapples with anxiousness yet deals with their anxiety by trying to avoid those feelings instead of expressing them. And those who tend more toward an anxious style are avoidant of tolerating their own uncomfortable feelings, so they act them out with their partner. Plus, those who basically operate out of a secure attachment style will sometimes behave in anxious or avoidant ways, and vice versa. Your style may vary in different relationships or under different circumstances. Thankfully, if you tend toward an insecure style that causes problems in your relationship, you can change. Plus, both of you can become more secure together.

Why is it helpful to learn about your own and your partner's attachment style? When things aren't going well in a disagreement, your awareness that attachment fears or issues are getting triggered for one or both of you helps you pause, gain perspective, not take your partner's behavior so personally, and feel more compassion for yourself and for them. This awareness also provides an opportunity to intervene in the habitual effort to get your attachment needs met by your mate and, instead, encourages you to turn inward to discern what's activated inside of you and try your best to self-soothe.[*]

Your differences—including different ways of handling conflicts—contribute to the frequency and intensity of your fights.

If you find yourself mired in repetitive patterns with an attachment flavor, you may benefit from working with a relationship coach or couples therapist trained in attachment issues. For a deeper dive into the impact of attachment styles on romantic relationships, read or listen to Dr. Sue Johnson's book, *Hold Me Tight*.

Even more factors contribute to Fighting Wrong, and they predate the arrival of your baby and are unique to you as individuals and to your relationship together. Innate differences sometimes heighten conflicts, such as whether individuals are extroverted or introverted, high energy or calm, spontaneous or slow to shift gears, gregarious or soft-spoken, and neurotypical or neurodivergent. While the adage "opposites attract"

---

[*] See Tools 28 through 31 for self-soothing insights and tips.

often holds true, your differences—including different ways of handling conflict—contribute to the frequency and intensity of your fights.

QUICK QUESTIONS

- What attachment style fits you most?
- How do you think your attachment style impacts how you fight with your spouse?
- What innate differences contribute to negative conflict between you and your partner?

CHAPTER 8

What if You Come from a Family or Culture of Fighters and Your Spouse Doesn't (or Vice Versa)?

For some of us, debate and engaged disagreements offer familiar ways to communicate with loved ones; for others, those approaches feel foreign or threatening. Your family of origin (including your epigenetic heritage), cultural and religious influences, temperament, and other life experiences impact your familiarity, as well as comfort or discomfort, with fighting, including Fighting Wrong.

Relationship problems often arise when spouses grow up with divergent conflict styles, such as when one of you is comfortable with or even welcomes arguing, while the other avoids raising or discussing contentious issues. For example, Latin, Middle Eastern, African American, and Jewish cultures often accommodate debate and impassioned conversations, including those with raised voices, spontaneous interruptions, and dramatic gestures. By contrast, Scandinavian and British cultures tend to be quieter and more restrained and may orient

> *Relationship problems often arise when spouses grow up with divergent conflict styles.*

more toward conflict avoidance. When people with contrasting backgrounds pair up, it is important to recognize that neither style is the "right" way to communicate.

Challenges still arise even if you both grew up in families where conflict and raised voices were accepted. While you may enjoy a good, heated debate, if the style of arguing that you learned as kids damages your connection, it will benefit from fine-tuning. Bottom line: Learning new and positive ways to Fight Right helps your relationship and your children's wellbeing.

CHAPTER 9

Why Are You Fighting More Now?

Because there is so much more to fight about! When your baby arrives, you experience new stressors, a steep learning curve, and new responsibilities. Usually, parenthood means you have less money, less time, less sleep, and less energy for intimacy. At the same time, you have more tasks to manage and divvy up and more complicated relationships with extended family.

You are learning the huge, complex role of parenting and figuring out how to share that role with your spouse. Plus, you may be grieving the loss of your partner's singular attention—after all, you now share priority with the baby— and that loss can breed resentment.*

Research shows that people who are sleep deprived are more likely to experience depressed feelings, anxiety, and hostility.

Let's unpack the impact of sleep deprivation a little more. Research shows that people who are sleep deprived are more likely to experience depressed feelings, anxiety, and hostility. They are less likely to feel grateful, have empathy for

---

* See Tool 27, Honor Your Transition to Parenthood, for more information on this topic.

others, or make good decisions. One study found a bidirectional connection between sleep and relationship quality: The better participants slept, the higher their relationship satisfaction; the more poorly they slept, the lower their relationship satisfaction. Similar results appeared in a study of new parents, in which more sleep corresponded to higher postpartum relationship fulfillment.

Since some degree of sleep deprivation is inevitable with a new baby, you might think, "What's the point of learning this? We can't do anything about it!" Yet increasing your awareness of the effects of sleep deprivation can be helpful in any number of ways:

- If you take a step back and acknowledge that some of the negativity you feel toward your partner (or they feel toward you), is caused by exhaustion, then you gain perspective. Perspective helps you avoid jumping to conclusions about how bad your relationship is or how much you can't stand your spouse.
- You can use that perspective to ask for a constructive "time-out," perhaps by saying, "I'm too tired to deal with this right now. Can we talk about it in the morning when, hopefully, I feel more rested?"
- Perspective also helps with repair, e.g., "Honey, I think neither of us was at our best when we got into that fight last night, and I'm sorry I was so reactive and defensive. How about we start fresh with that discussion?"
- Realizing that sleep deprivation hugely affects your relationship and your perception of it will also help you prioritize getting more sleep!

Understanding that the stressors of new parenthood contribute to increased conflict—and normalizing that increase, at least for a while—lessens the sting of Fighting Wrong, encourages compassion, and eases your adjustment to life with a baby.

PART THREE

Five Common Areas of Conflict and How to Better Handle Them

This section focuses on five common areas of conflict among new parents and provides the tools to navigate them. The five areas of conflict are: 1) money, 2) division of labor, 3) gatekeeping and parenting styles, 4) sex and intimacy, and 5) in-laws and extended family.

Because one size doesn't fit all when it comes to relationships, we offer multiple ways to resolve the same issue. Your learning style might differ from that of your partner, one or both of you might prefer certain tools over others, one tool might assist the first time you try it but not the next, and some tools might prove more effective in your relationship than others. Most tools apply to conflicts across topics, including those not covered in this book, so feel free to mix and match and apply tools as you see fit.

CHAPTER 10

Money

Money is a hot-button topic for most relationships and often sparks disagreements about spending and saving philosophies, habits, and priorities. Finances trigger challenging questions and choices: Do we have enough? How can we get more? Who should earn it? How can we reduce debt? Save more? What should we spend money on? What should we not spend it on? Who should pay the bills?

Disagreements about money escalate easily. Why? Because they touch on core issues, beliefs, and feelings that are often emotionally charged. When it comes to financial conflict, many people hold contrasting perspectives and beliefs about money.

What follows is a list of polarities commonly tied to money in our culture. Review them to clarify the meanings you and your partner attribute to money and to deepen your understanding of your similarities and differences.

+ Control and lack of control
+ Power and powerlessness
+ Freedom and structure
+ Risk and safety
+ Independence and dependence
+ Success and failure
+ Competence and incompetence

+ Worthiness and unworthiness
+ Generosity and frugality
+ Security and vulnerability
+ Predictability and spontaneity
+ Responsibility and irresponsibility

Understanding the influence of your and your partner's childhood experiences on your current financial styles can be enlightening and empowering. Another way to enhance understanding is to consider how your family of origin influenced your financial attitudes.

Do any of these scenarios sound familiar to you or your spouse?

+ You grew up in a family that expressed love with gift-giving or generous allowances.
+ Your family faced poverty, so money was tied to survival instincts, safety, and security.
+ Your parents' financial struggles were embarrassing to them—and, perhaps, you—so the lack of money was a source of shame.
+ Your parents' generosity sometimes felt like a substitute for—not an expression of—their love and affection.
+ Your family avoided discussing money, so that topic was taboo.
+ Your parents' ability to buy certain things sparked pride and a sense of achievement.
+ Your family prioritized saving as an expression of caring and love.
+ Your parents' passion for saving felt withholding or punishing.

✦ One of your parents controlled the family finances, while the other seemed dependent, inept, or resentful about money.

QUICK QUESTIONS

Whether or not any of those scenarios closely match your experience, consider:

- How would you describe your family dynamic around money?
- How do your childhood experiences inform your approach to money now?
- How do they impact your relationship with your spouse around finances?

Some people replicate their parents' financial strategies to maintain the status quo, honor the family legacy, or express respect and appreciation for their parents' struggles and values. Others reject the financial philosophies with which they were raised to differentiate themselves from their family, explore their own attitudes toward money, or rebel against parental authority. While these responses are common, unless you know whether any of them influences you and unless you take time to discuss that influence with your spouse, your past might inadvertently contribute to negative conflict and financial misunderstandings in the present.

Your past might inadvertently contribute to negative conflict and financial misunderstandings in the present.

Preexisting individual debt also stresses relationships. Throw a baby into the mix—which adds expenses, often in combination with less income if parents take time off from work—and money troubles often become money conflicts.

Here are four tools to help you resolve financial disagreements:

 ## TOOL 1. WHAT IF WE'RE BOTH RIGHT?

This simple question offers a powerful paradigm shift to help you and your partner get unstuck. Asking it with an open mind changes the channel in your brain from win-lose to win-win.

Like other differences of opinion, discussions about finances often feel like showdowns between the right way (yours) and the wrong way (theirs). Yet most spending and saving styles are tied to subjective opinions, preferences, habits, feelings, strategies, thoughts, and beliefs about money rather than objective measures.

If you tackle financial differences by posing the question "What if we're both right?" you shift from a face-off about whose philosophy is correct to a discussion based on acceptance and understanding.

As noted in Guiding Principle #7, there are key differences between understanding and agreeing. Understanding suggests that you "get" (comprehend) that your spouse's approach to finances reflects their values and priorities. Understanding means that even if you don't share their philosophy or don't agree that their approach offers the best way to address money, you respect and accept the validity of their viewpoint. Importantly, the willingness to understand your partner's perspective does not mean you agree with it or that you abandon your preferred financial strategy.

By contrast, agreeing with your beloved means that you share the same approach to finances and that their monetary philosophy aligns with your own. While agreeing is great, it's not necessary to resolve financial (or other types of) struggles.

The more you accept that your spouse's approach to money has merit—meaning, the more you understand their perspective—the more you can compromise productively and navigate differences around finances respectfully.

The more you accept that your spouse's approach to money has merit, the more you can compromise productively.

This ties in nicely with Tool 2: Money Types. For example, *The Pleasure Seeker* balances *The Saver*: "Yes, we want to prioritize saving but not to such an extreme that we miss out on experiences in the present."

QUICK QUESTIONS

- What's important to you about your approach to money?
- How do you think your approach serves your family?
- If you're both right, how can you negotiate financial decisions without judgment or negative conflict?

 ## TOOL 2. MONEY TYPES

Spencer Sherman and Brent Kessel, authors of the online course *Money and Spirit*, created a useful self-assessment tool to identify financial styles and values.[3] Their Financial Archetypes increase self-knowledge, enhance understanding of your mate's approach, and give you a new angle on resolving money conflicts. If you understand that your spouse's financial style is part of their personality and not just some random reaction or opposition to your approach, then you will find it easier to communicate respectfully about money topics.

Financial Archetypes describe traits or tendencies. You might recognize yourself primarily in one archetype or possibly in all eight, or you might come up with additional types of your own. Financial Archetypes provide a basis for understanding how you arrived at your current financial life and a way to become more conscious and intentional in crafting a financial plan together.

Here are the eight archetypes:

1. *The Guardian* is alert and careful.
2. *The Pleasure Seeker* prioritizes pleasure and enjoyment in the here and now.
3. *The Idealist* places the greatest value on creativity, compassion, social justice, or spiritual growth.
4. *The Saver* seeks security and abundance by accumulating more financial assets.
5. *The Star* spends, invests, or gives money away to be recognized, feel hip or classy, and increase self-esteem.
6. *The Innocent* avoids putting significant attention on money and believes or hopes that life will work out for the best.

7. *The Caretaker* gives and lends money to express compassion and generosity.

8. *The Empire Builder* thrives on power and innovation to create something of enduring value.

None of these archetypes is good or bad. Each is potentially useful *and* problematic. Each one is a double-edged sword. For example, while *The Guardian* remains alert and careful with money, which facilitates saving, a person with this archetype can take it to an extreme and become rigid or what people criticize as "a tightwad."

Understanding your financial tendencies—especially if they are inflexible or extreme—creates an opportunity to explore financial styles and traits that don't come naturally to you, thereby developing a more balanced approach. You and your partner can support each other in this growth process. Just reviewing the list of Financial Archetypes and sharing insights together can open up new ways for you and your mate to discuss finances and honor your similarities and differences.

 ## TOOL 3. LET'S MAKE A DEAL

This tool introduces levity into money disagreements. You and your beloved playfully invite each other to "make a deal" around finances.

Strategies include:

+   Meet somewhere in the middle.
+   Let one person's money style lead one time and defer to the other when the next issue arises.
+   Negotiate compromises.
+   Explore hybrid solutions.

For example, let's say your spouse wants a $1,000 stroller, and you think the $200 one is already pricey. A meet-some-where-in-the-middle strategy might look like this: "I think the $200 stroller is adequate for our needs. Then again, I know you want to jog with the baby, and the more expensive one has the best wheels and shock absorption. How about we compromise and purchase the $600 model, which got good reviews from parents who like to run?"

Get creative and craft your own hybrid deals. To continue the stroller example: "If I agree to the more expensive stroller, which would support your preferred way to exercise, would you agree to my getting a gym membership?" The essence of this tool is to lighten up and craft productive ways to compromise.

QUICK QUESTIONS

- If you think of compromise as collaborative and helpful—instead of a recipe for unexpressed resentment—what are you willing to compromise around money?
- If you accept that sometimes you need to give something to get something, what new options arise?
- What might be a win-win solution to this conflict, even if only a partial win?

 ## TOOL 4. THE GOOD START TOOL

One of the simplest ways to address money differences—and other differences, too—is to ensure that your conversation begins well. Positive beginnings often precipitate positive outcomes. The three primary components to starting conversations well are: respectful word choice, open body language, and vocal tone and energy that convey your genuine interest in the other person's perspective.

> **One of the simplest ways to address money differences—is to ensure that your conversation begins well.**

Here are tips to ensure a good start to your discussion:

+ Before you sit down together, take a minute to imagine how you want your chat to end. Think about how you want to feel when it's over, how you want your beloved to feel, and how you want to feel together. Allow this best-case scenario to inform how you show up.
+ Scan your body for tight or stressed spots and for resentful or other negative feelings toward your partner. Spend a few moments breathing into those constricted areas and emotions, with a view to loosening or releasing them. Begin your conversation as relaxed as possible.
+ Assume you both have valid points instead of assuming you're right and they're wrong.
+ Speak from the "I" instead of focusing on "you," and use open and flexible language—I believe, I think, I feel, I wonder, I hope, I wish—in lieu of I know, I'm certain, and I'm correct.

✦ Consider going one step further and use tentative language: "I'm not sure, yet I think . . .," "I don't know if I'm correct, though I believe . . .," and "You might have a different perspective. I want to hear yours and share mine."

✦ Let your mate know what's important to you about your perspective on this particular issue and get curious about what's important to them.

✦ Be aware of your posture and body language. Try to sit in a way that reflects openness: Uncross your arms, gently lean toward your spouse, maintain eye contact, and keep a respectful distance between you.

Integrating as many of these suggestions as possible into your conversation about finances will enhance your skill set for Fighting Right and help your discussion begin and conclude well, even if you still disagree.

CHAPTER 11

Division of Labor

Conflict about who does what—including housework, yard-work, shopping, and managing finances—is common for everyone who cohabits. Becoming parents often intensifies the charge around the division of labor by adding an over-whelming number of new tasks. Many parents get caught in a "who has it worse" cycle by trying to establish who is more exhausted, who works harder, or who has the more difficult or important roles.

> **Becoming parents often intensifies the charge around the division of labor by adding an overwhelming number of new tasks.**

Heterosexual relationships, in particular, often rely on—or revert to—traditional gender roles when a baby arrives, which means that most heterosexual women—including those who work outside the home—perform more than half the housework and child-care tasks than their spouses. Research suggests that when heterosexual mothers' prenatal expectations don't match what they perceive as the fathers' postpartum efforts—i.e., when moms think dads do less than they said they would or than those moms believed they would—their relationship satisfaction suffers.

Invisible and emotional labor further impede an equitable distribution of tasks. Invisible labor consists of household- and family-related work performed by one person that doesn't register on the other's radar. Emotional labor refers to the mental energy expended to maintain the health and wellbeing of relationships, of individuals in those relationships—especially children—and of a household. Invisible and emotional labor are sometimes interdependent and often spark feelings of being put-upon, unappreciated, lonely, or abandoned.

Emotional and invisible labor take many forms. For example, you might insist on doing all the laundry and refuse to wait until your partner decides to help with this task (if they ever do) because you hold the emotional labor of anticipating your baby's needs, including their frequent outfit changes, and of keeping your household running smoothly. Your spouse, too, might be handling more than you realize. For example, their resistance to buying another play swing for the baby might result from the invisible labor of tracking expenses and making sure there are adequate funds to pay the bills.

Invisible and emotional labor become especially burdensome when one person shoulders—or believes they shoulder—much more of it, when the pressure and impact of that labor remain unarticulated or unexplored, or when one of you is unaware of or insensitive to the invisible or emotional labor the other person manages.

Whether related to invisible and emotional labor or not, Fighting Wrong about who does what creates a lose-lose scenario. Explore these tools to shift to win-win.[*]

---

[*] To explore new parents' division of labor in greater detail and to plan for, or shift to, greater equity, see the Who-Does-What Exercise at https://rhonaberens.com/who-does-what-exercise/.

 ## TOOL 5. WHAT'S YOUR HEART'S DESIRE?

Complaining about your partner's failure to pull her weight, or his unreasonable expectations, often *feels* justified. Yet complaints are like artichoke leaves. There might be a little meat on them, yet they're mostly prickly and bare.

Taking the artichoke metaphor further: As you pull off those thorny leaves, think of the fuzz that covers the artichoke heart as the fears and worries attached to your complaints. Your fears and worries take shape in phrases like "I'm afraid I'll have to do it all," "I'm worried our baby will suffer if something falls through the cracks," "I'm already barely getting by at my job, so I don't have anything more to give at home," "I'm afraid that I'll never satisfy you," or "There's not enough time for me!"

All of these are valid concerns. Yet if you solely focus on concerns, worries, or fears, you will probably keep locking horns with your mate and miss the big picture of what matters most: the core of your complaint.

To get to that core, think of the heart of an artichoke—that juicy, delicious center—as a dream, yearning, longing, goal, wish, hope, or desire that you fear, or believe, is under threat. Examples include a wish to be a great parent, a longing to be part of a loving and collaborative parenting team, a hope to rest more, a goal to succeed at a job *and* as a parent, a yearning for recognition of what you do and not what you fail to do, or a desire to let someone else take the lead.

The more you start conversations by naming your desires, wishes, or goals—instead of leading with complaints, criticisms, or fears—the more likely your beloved will be to understand not only what's not working for you but why it's not working. Then they can respond with empathy and without defensiveness. In the best-case scenario, increased understanding helps you get your needs met wholly, or at least partially. Regardless of tangible outcomes, increased understanding contributes to mutual respect and positive compromise.

QUICK QUESTIONS

- What dream or goal do you believe is threatened, or perhaps already destroyed, because of the issue you're complaining about?
- How can you describe that dream, desire, wish, or hope to your spouse without defensiveness, blame, or contempt?
- How can you ask for support, and better support yourself, to get your wish(es) met, if only partially?

TOOL 6. SWITCH ROLES

When caught up in reactivity or judgment, we often lose touch with our vulnerability. The same holds true for our partners. Many people are uncomfortable acknowledging their vulnerability and tend to forget their spouse's tender spots when they Fight Wrong. Opening up that part of you, though sometimes scary, creates space to connect with each other as lovable and fallible humans with valid needs, and it increases your ability to relate lovingly to each other.

Switching roles is an effective and often fun way to tap into that vulnerability, increase empathy for your mate, and step outside your subjective position on a conflict. Role-play also offers an opportunity to imagine the invisible or emotional labor your spouse experiences, especially if they complain that you don't recognize their efforts.

When you feel stuck and polarized and find yourselves repeating things over and over, try switching roles. One of you might say, "I'm noticing that we're not getting anywhere with the way we're talking about this. What if I pretend to be you and you pretend to be me, and we switch sides temporarily to see how that feels?"

The premise is that you each genuinely do your best to describe and respectfully argue your spouse's perspective as if it were your own, including by offering compelling reasons for why your partner's perspective is right. This involves imagining their experience as *they* see it, not as how you want them to see it or think they should see it.

Even if you believe they're only 5 percent or 10 percent right, argue as if you're 100 percent convinced of their perspective. Commit temporarily to letting go of your own point of view. This process will only help if done respectfully and with a genuine intent to express your beloved's position and understand the reasons behind it.

Here are suggested steps for this exercise:

1. Spend a minute or two thinking about your spouse's perspective without arguing against it inside your head. Your job is to consider what they value and feel, what need or wish they hope to fulfill, and what they are trying to express to you.

2. Decide who will go first as the Role-Player and who will be the Listener.

3. Set a timer for three minutes.

4. As the Role-Player, present your mate's perspective with genuine effort and compassion. If your partner often uses critical, blaming, or defensive language about this issue, shift to neutral or positive terms. Consider what yearning lies beneath their harsh words. No worries if you take less than three minutes; however, effectively conveying their perspective should take more than a few seconds.

5. The job of the Listener is to just hear what the Role-Player is saying.

6. After the timer goes off or the Role-Player finishes talking, whichever comes first, the Role-Player should ask the Listener, "What would you like to add to or revise in what I said?"

7. Listener, please keep your response brief and polite.

8. Reset the timer and switch places as Role-Player and Listener. Repeat steps four through seven.

9. If you're both eager to discuss what you just learned about yourself and each other, do so now. If one or both of you prefers to digest this exercise before discussing it, schedule a time to revisit this issue in the next day or two.

You may be surprised by the insights gained about yourself, your spouse, and your relationship by switching roles. If you prefer, feel free to complete this exercise in writing, including asking and responding in writing to the following questions:

QUICK QUESTIONS

- What was it like to genuinely convey my perspective on this issue?
- What did you learn by playing my part?
- What did you learn about yourself by listening to me play your part?
- If both our perspectives are valid, where do we go from here?

TOOL 7. ACKNOWLEDGMENTS AND APPRECIATIONS

Everyone likes to feel appreciated and have their efforts and perspectives acknowledged. Appreciations and acknowledgments often inspire cooperation and action, and they spotlight emotional or invisible labor that otherwise goes unnamed and unrecognized.

Intentionally nurture and reinforce positive feedback until it becomes a new habit.

If your feedback focuses on failures, you can count on getting the same kind of response in return. Criticism is rarely a positive motivator; instead, it breeds resentment, defensiveness, or withdrawal. Because the human brain has an inherent negativity bias—a tendency to look for and dwell on what's wrong and to react unproductively to negative comments or words—it helps to intentionally nurture and reinforce positive feedback until it becomes a new habit.

Acknowledgments and appreciations offer quick ways to support Fighting Right. If your partner complains that they do the laundry more often than you, try to curb your defensiveness or criticism—or intervene in stonewalling by not withdrawing—and, instead, lead with where you agree. For example: "Thank you so much for doing the laundry. I really appreciate your efforts." By acknowledging what you *do* agree with, you avoid escalating the conflict.

Effective appreciations are specific and tailored to the other person's strengths, so try to avoid generic, rote expressions of gratitude. Those often come across as phony. To ensure your comment lands, it needs to be distinct and genuine. Saying "great job" sounds nice yet vague. "You're so good at making bath time fun!" offers more detail for the person on the receiving end.

The best expressions of gratitude are personalized and speak to your partner's priorities and challenges, such as "I know you were concerned about spending the day alone with the baby, but you were a rock star!" or "I know it's hard to find time to do the laundry, which is why I'm especially grateful you made it a priority."

Here are a few catchphrases to help you tell your spouse what they do well:

- ✦ Thank you for . . .
- ✦ I'm so grateful that . . .
- ✦ I noticed when you . . .
- ✦ You're so skilled at . . .
- ✦ I really appreciate that you . . .
- ✦ You excel at . . .
- ✦ It helps so much that you . . .
- ✦ The baby loves it when you . . .

To further motivate you to practice acknowledgments and appreciations, consider Dr. John Gottman's finding that the ratio of positive to negative interactions is one of the most accurate predictors of relationship success or failure. His "magic ratio" of what supports a stable and fulfilling relationship is 5 to 1 positive to negative interactions, so feel free to catch your spouse doing things well as often as possible.

 ## TOOL 8. SHARE THE STORY

Do you ever make up a story about what's going on inside your partner's mind? Then, without confirming it, you act or react as if it were true? Many of us do!

Even if you're often right in presuming to know your spouse's thoughts or emotions, a "know it all" is tough to live with. Plus, those times when you're wrong, yet act or react as if you're right, damage mutual trust and respect. Acting as if you know your mate's thoughts and feelings, without checking in, suggests you have nothing new to learn about them, which is never the case. This is a good time to remind yourself: "Don't believe everything I think!" or "Just because I think it doesn't make it true!"

Bringing stories out into the open helps to reduce negative conflict. For example, you might say, "When you don't clean up after mealtime, the story I tell myself is that you just assume I'll do it." Your partner might offer a new story by sharing that they were exhausted from the day and planned to clean up after the baby's bedtime. Or they might admit that was exactly what they were thinking and either take responsibility and apologize, or not. Either way, by honestly sharing your thoughts, you open space to discuss and resolve the issue and create new and more accurate stories.

Nonverbal cues also inspire stories. Your spouse's facial expressions, posture, or silence get interpreted, for example, as disapproval or judgment. Instead of believing your story, ask them what they are thinking or feeling. Perhaps your interpretation is correct; perhaps their facial expression and feelings don't match; perhaps they switched gears internally to another topic; perhaps they zoned out. While the last two responses aren't ideal, they differ from your original story and potentially open space for a new discussion, e.g., the impact of sleep deprivation on the ability to focus.

QUICK QUESTIONS

- What story are you making up about this issue right now?
- What new possibilities might emerge if you share your story with your partner to determine its accuracy?
- What new stories might be possible if yours isn't 100 percent true?
- What new, positive stories might you create together?

CHAPTER 12

Gatekeeping and Contrasting Parenting Styles

Disagreements often occur when you and your spouse differ about key parenting decisions and, in response, one of you engages in gatekeeping. We define gatekeeping as a territorial power struggle in which one of you does any or all of the following:

+ Feels and acts entitled to more control over certain parenting decisions or actions.
+ Prevents or discourages your beloved from making their own parenting choices, including mistakes.
+ Criticizes your partner repeatedly, which sometimes leads to that person giving up on a task or on engaging as a parent altogether.
+ Monitors or blocks your mate's interactions with the baby.

Gatekeeping shows up around common, everyday tasks, such as claiming there's only one right way to burp the baby, as well as specific decisions, such as insisting you select the babysitter because you know the baby's needs better than your spouse.

Gatekeeping can be toxic not only by causing conflict but also by interfering with each parent developing their own unique relationship with the baby and building trust in themselves as a parent. In heterosexual couples, when there is a stay-at-home mom and a dad who works full time outside the home, the stay-at-home parent is more likely to fall into gatekeeping tendencies, e.g., "Since I'm the one breastfeeding and spending so much more time with our baby, I know his needs better than you."

While there might be limited truth to that claim, parenting—including the right to make key decisions—is based on more than time spent with your child. Just think about parents who work outside the home. No one believes that a babysitter, daycare worker, or extended family member who spends many hours tending to a baby has more or even as much of a right as parents to make crucial decisions about that child's wellbeing or future. All parents, including working parents, retain that right.

Parents often lock horns because parenting styles, strategies, and decisions differ.

Even if neither of you gatekeeps, parents often lock horns because parenting styles, strategies, and decisions differ. The four tools in this section help new parents capably navigate, decrease, and avoid gatekeeping and find respectful ways to accommodate differences in parenting philosophies.

TOOL 9. WHAT'S IMPORTANT TO YOU ABOUT THAT?

Sometimes a simple question powerfully shifts a conversation from negative conflict to greater closeness. When asked from a place of genuine curiosity, the question "What's important to you about that?" opens a discussion, sparks deeper exploration, and dissolves resentment. Like other powerful questions (such as Tool 1: What If We're Both Right?), "What's important to you about that?" opens up surprising possibilities.

To illustrate, let's imagine a couple in which the mom is the primary caregiver. The parents disagree about when to switch the baby's car seat from backward facing to forward facing. If gatekeeping dominates their interaction, when she finds out her husband turned the car seat around before a long drive home, she might say with a critical and controlling tone: "I know best, and safety is the most important thing. I can't believe you put our baby at risk!"

If the mom asks, "What's important to you about that?" *before* she launches into criticizing her spouse, he might share that he was feeling frantic and unable to focus while driving because the baby was screaming and spitting up, both of which stopped when he turned the seat around and interacted more easily with her from the front. Dad might share his history of getting carsick as a child and his empathy for their baby, who might feel isolated and nauseous because of facing backward.

The mom might still believe that safety overrides the dad's concerns, yet by checking in with her mate first, she can follow up respectfully, acknowledge his point of view, and ask for further discussion because of her lingering concerns. This couple can then recognize that each of their perspectives is important, and they both want what is best for their baby, even if they differ in how to achieve that.

For the gatekeeping parent, the goal is to use discernment about when to intervene in response to your beloved's parenting decisions. A good rule of thumb is to "bite your tongue" unless urgent health or safety concerns are involved. Even if those concerns come up, as in the car seat example, avoid communicating in a disrespectful way or undermining your partner's confidence in their parenting.

If you are on the receiving end of gatekeeping, the goal is neither to endure your spouse's efforts to control and manipulate your parenting or access to your baby, nor to fight tooth and nail for your way of doing things. Instead, try to better understand why your partner is acting that way and what they're trying to accomplish or prevent. Letting them know you understand their perspective helps them hear yours and helps you stand your ground from a place of kindness instead of resentment or defensiveness.

A variation of this exercise is to integrate what's important to you into *your* side of a conversation. Even without being asked, explain to your spouse that "It's important to me to spend more time alone caring for our baby so that she feels safe with me, and I feel more confident as her parent." This approach lets you take the reins of the conversation instead of waiting for your partner to get curious.

QUICK QUESTIONS

- How might your child benefit if you relax your grip on parenting?
- How might your relationship improve if you loosen your gatekeeping efforts?
- How might your parenting improve if you respectfully refuse your mate's gatekeeping and assert your desire to explore your own way of doing things?
- What might you learn if you get curious about your differences in parenting styles?

TOOL 10. NORMALIZE CONFLICT

Normalizing is a simple tool that reduces the charge and intensity of conflict and the tendency to blame yourself or your spouse. By acknowledging how common negative conflict is and how unavoidable it is to disagree, especially after becoming parents, you diffuse or lessen its destructive impact on you and your relationship.

Compare these examples and imagine how each would land with you or your partner:

+ "It shouldn't be this hard! You're always disagreeing with my opinions about how to take care of the baby. Maybe we shouldn't have had a child together!"
+ "This is hard, and I know we're not alone. It makes sense that we disagree more now. Let's take a step back and try to remember this is a challenging time for *all* new parents."

While the first response is common, it's also demoralizing and destructive. It implies there's something wrong with you, your spouse, or your relationship, which makes it isolating and personal. By normalizing conflict, the second response inspires understanding, connection, and collaboration. It reminds you that you are part of a larger community of new parents experiencing an increase in relationship conflict. Normalizing your struggles invites you to put Fighting Wrong in perspective and encourages optimism in your ability to manage and move past it.

You are part of a larger community of new parents experiencing an increase in relationship conflict.

 ## *TOOL 11. EXTERNALIZE THE PROBLEM*

This tool helps you access a bigger-picture perspective, which releases you from seeing each other as the problem or letting the problem come between you. Here, you view each other as allies who solve issues together.

As usual, the language you use matters. There's a big difference, for example, between finger-pointing—"You're screwing up bedtime again!"—and describing events in a more neutral way: "I'm noticing we're fighting again about the best way to put the baby to bed, and that pits us against each other. How can we collaborate and figure this out?"

You may need to remind yourself and each other of your shared goals—being teammates, your baby's health and well-being, your relationship satisfaction—that transcend differences of opinion. In this example, you both want and probably desperately need better sleep for your baby and yourselves. You just disagree on how to get there.

One powerful way to play this out is to literally externalize the problem by choosing an object to represent it. Here are step-by-step instructions to do so, with bedtime as the example:

1. Choose a neutral object from your home, preferably one with corners or edges like a box, and tape a note to it that names the issue you're battling about, in this case, "Bedtime Routine."

2. Sit next to your spouse and place that object between you so that you're both pressed against it, though not uncomfortably so.

3. Acknowledge that, right now, this issue is literally a wedge between you, separating you from each other and from the ability to work together to resolve it.

4. Together, walk that object across the room and place it on the floor or another surface.

5. Return to your seats and sit with one leg pressed gently against your spouse's leg.

6. Together, look at the object across the room and acknowledge that you are the best team to figure out how to resolve that issue and that doing so depends on being gentle with and connected to each other.

7. From this perspective, brainstorm possible solutions to this issue, with the understanding that none is right or wrong.

8. If you notice tensions rising, the issue is likely separating you again. Retrieve the object, place it between you again for a few moments, and when you both feel ready to collaborate, walk it back across the room so you can return to being teammates.

9. Discuss the options you brainstormed with a view to finding one, or a combination, that you're both willing to try.

By the way, this particular topic—bedtime for your baby—generates huge disagreements among parenting experts. If professionals disagree on the best bedtime routine, trying to convince your partner that your way is the only way is doomed to fail. While experts generally agree on some parenting issues—for example, those in North America believe that corporal punishment negatively impacts children's health and wellbeing into adulthood—many topics have less consensus, including sleep training or when to introduce bottle-feeding.

 ## TOOL 12. THE THIRD THING

It's all too easy to get locked into a parenting battle in which you believe you only have two choices: your approach or theirs. So, whatever the outcome, one of you will get your way and the other will not. Winner-loser. Simple as that.

More often than you think, you can find a "third thing," a third solution that emerges *if* you both take a step back and open your minds.

For example, imagine that a lesbian couple has chosen to start a family, and for the most part, both women eagerly await the baby's arrival. Yet every time they talk about sleeping arrangements, tensions build. One mom-to-be envisions the family bed, all three of them sleeping together, cozy and intimate. To her beloved, this sounds like a recipe for sleepless nights and no privacy. She wants the baby in a crib in another room. Both feel strongly about what they want. Both seem locked into their position and determined to get their way . . . until friends share their creative solution to a similar stalemate: They use a co-sleeper that attaches to the bed, which gives the couple their own sleeping space. Plus, they have a crib in another room for times when they want more privacy. The co-sleeper with a crib in another room is the "third thing" they can both accept.

Take a moment to consider areas of conflict between you and your spouse where you both dig in and stubbornly defend your positions. Share the "third thing" concept with your mate and suggest you both take a step back, make space to view the problem with a bigger-picture lens that allows for more creativity, and then brainstorm together. You could also invite a neutral third party to weigh in with ideas. You may be pleasantly surprised by what emerges.

CHAPTER 13

Sex and Intimacy

There are good reasons so many clichés and jokes circulate after a baby arrives about never having sex again. To begin with, new parents simply don't have as much time, energy, or privacy as before. Add in hormonal changes for a mom who just gave birth,[4] and sleep deprivation for all parents, including those who adopt or foster, and sex easily becomes a battlefield or the Holy Grail.

Realistic expectations help. Romance, intimacy, and your sexual relationship will change. Period. Yet realism isn't the same as pessimism; even as your sex life shifts—perhaps briefly, perhaps for a long time, even perhaps for the better— that doesn't mean you'll *never* have satisfying or passionate sex again. This is not the time for black-and-white, all-or-nothing, always-or-never thinking. In other words, don't throw the baby out with the bathwater!

Given that sex and intimacy are sometimes charged even before you become parents, better understanding your own assumptions and triggers, and sharing them with your beloved, decreases the likelihood of Fighting Wrong. It also opens the door to deeper connection and sensitivity with each other and more satisfying sexual experiences.

As with conflicts regarding money, fights about sex and intimacy are often heated and complex because core beliefs, emotions, and old wounds get triggered. Unskilled conflicts about sex or intimacy often center on one or more of the following issues: power, desirability, worthiness, security, performance, closeness, commitment, trust, freedom, safety, reciprocity, and pleasure. No matter which issue(s) triggers you or how it does so—for example, you might get activated because you want your partner to express their desire for you, or you might get triggered when expressing your desire for them—sex and intimacy offer insights into who you are and what turns you on.

To deepen your intimacy with yourself and your spouse, take note of which of the issues listed in the previous paragraph resonate for you in your relationship. Then, consider exploring these questions with your partner. Do your best to listen with compassion and without reactivity to their feelings and yearnings, and call forth your courage to express your own feelings and yearnings as well.

QUICK QUESTIONS

- How does that issue affect your expectations around sex or intimacy, whether of yourself or your mate?
- How does parenthood intensify some of those issues?
- How might respectfully sharing your perspectives on those issues benefit your relationship?

Please note that if you are someone with a history of sexual abuse, then intimacy and sex might already be a fraught terrain for you and your relationship, and giving birth can be retraumatizing. If that scenario applies, the tools in this section might not provide enough support to help you and your relationship reignite postpartum sex and intimacy. We encourage you to seek additional help.[*]

Fights about sex and intimacy are often heated and complex because core beliefs, emotions, and old wounds get triggered.

In this chapter, we invite you to embrace your new reality as parents while honoring the continued importance of sex and intimacy to your wellbeing, both individually and in your relationship.

Practice the following Tools 13-16 to keep the good kind of postpartum sparks flying.

TOOL 13. SELF-NURTURING ALONE TIME

If you're a new parent recovering from birth, nurturing yourself—and pampering your postpartum body—often falls to the wayside. This might seem like an inconvenient time to do so; however, taking a few minutes to explore your body in a sensual way—meaning, gently and kindly being present to your body and the ways in which it feels the same as and different than before you gave birth—is important.

Why take time to connect with your body now, given how little time you have to do even the most basic of things, like showering and brushing your hair? Because your sensory

---

* See Part 5 for more information.

experiences can help you feel better physically and emotionally. Plus, if you remain disconnected from your body, it will be that much harder to connect intimately with your spouse. How can you reconnect to yourself?

Here are a few suggestions:

+ Take a candlelit bath.
+ Ask your partner or a friend for a hand, neck, or shoulder massage.
+ Get a manicure or pedicure.
+ Rub your favorite lotion on your body.
+ Try a few basic yoga poses or stretches.
+ Walk on the grass in your bare feet.
+ Take time in the shower to focus on the sensation of the water on your skin.
+ Gently touch your body to familiarize yourself with how it feels now.

The important purpose is to tune into or discover what feels good to your postpartum self. Develop the habit of asking: "What does my body want right now, at this moment?" It might be the smallest thing, like realizing you have to go to the bathroom and have been putting it off or that heating up your cup of coffee will enhance your enjoyment of it. Paying attention to your physical signals creates a more embodied experience for you, which means increased awareness of pain and discomfort *and* pleasure and comfort.

Do something, anything, *that* reconnects you to your body.

Cultivate a kind attitude toward your body and appreciate all it has achieved, even if you can think of ways in which you wish it looked or felt different, even if parts of it feel unfamiliar and you're unsure how to reconcile the body you once knew—whether before or during pregnancy—with the one in which you now find yourself.

In other words: Do something, anything, that reconnects you to your body. Your partner, too, might benefit from physical self-nurturing, so feel free to encourage them to explore any or all of the suggestions above. The same holds true for adoptive and foster parents, as you, too, benefit from embodied self-care.

Too often, spouses try to sexually connect when disconnected from themselves. Exploring your own sensuality not only nurtures you, but it can also serve as foreplay to intimacy with each other.

TOOL 14. GET RID OF YOUR BUTS . . . RIGHT NOW

If you disagree about sex and intimacy, especially the topic of frequency, then a both/and approach can help. Begin by replacing the word "but" with the word "and." That's right, as often as possible, remove "but" from your vocabulary and use "and" instead.

The brain's negativity bias means that when most people hear the word "but," they focus solely on the words that follow it. Pretty much everything leading up to "but"—even the most endearing words and sentiments like "I love you," "I'm still attracted to you," "I want to make love with you," or "I miss sex with you"—either loses its meaning altogether or becomes *less* meaningful than what you say afterward, such as: "I'm not open to having sex," "I'm too tired for sex," "I can't deal with one more person touching me," or "The answer is no."

While a "but" divides you from your beloved, the word "and" maintains the connection, even if it is less connection than your spouse desires: "I'm still attracted to you, *and* I'm too tired for sex." If you want to further enhance your bond, consider adding the words "right now" at the end of your sentence: "I love you, and I'm not open to having sex *right now*," "I want to make love with you, and I can't deal with one more person touching me *right now*." Your partner might still be disappointed, yet they're far less likely to feel significantly rejected or hurt, which are common reactions to the word "but."

The same principle holds true if you want to be sexual and your spouse doesn't. Words like "I understand," "That makes sense," and "I hear you" lose their meaning—and bonding potential—when followed by "*but* what I want matters too," "*but* you promised we'd still be sexual after the baby arrived," "*but* it's hard to hear no," or "*but* I miss our sex life so much!" Again, replacing "but" with "and" allows you to express your feelings while also taking into consideration your partner's experience.

As simple as it sounds, changing your language—even a single word—can make all the difference between calmly discussing an issue and devolving into negative conflict. Contrasting sexual desires—whether that means differences in how often you want intimacy, what time of day you prefer to be sexual, what turns you on or off the most, or other discrepancies between you—exist in many relationships before parenthood and are even more likely postpartum. Respecting those differences, while also finding ways to connect intimately, offers benefits from a both/and approach instead of either/or because it honors the idea that you're both right instead of indicating that what one of you wants matters more than what the other desires.

# *TOOL 15. THE PLATINUM RULE*

We're all familiar with The Golden Rule: "Do unto others as you would have them do unto you." Understandably, many people believe that's the most loving way to treat your beloved. Have you heard of The Platinum Rule? "Do unto others as *they* would have you do unto *them*." The Platinum Rule acknowledges that you and your partner likely have different preferences regarding how you want to be treated.

When it comes to sex and intimacy—actually, when it comes to most areas of relationships—The Platinum Rule provides better guidance for connection and fulfillment than The Golden Rule. Of course, implementing this rule requires *knowing* how your spouse wishes to be treated, so ask and listen with an open mind and genuine curiosity.

The Platinum Rule can take various forms, including asking your beloved to touch you the way you most want to be touched, and vice versa. The following exercise provides an opportunity for you to consciously explore touch with playful curiosity and without pressure or expectation that it will lead to sex. It begins with you agreeing to *not* have sex, even if you feel open to it or *really, really* want it.

The absence of criticism or judgment is also crucial to this tool, so please remain as open as possible to what gets expressed. If criticism or judgment starts to creep in, ask for a quick break to return to a neutral place. If you struggle to return to a neutral mindset, ask yourself:

- ✦ What concerns me about my spouse's request?
- ✦ What am I worried might happen, or not happen, if I touch them in the way they desire?

Those questions help you explore the root of your discomfort. Doing so is important because another key ingredient of this exercise is to touch in ways that are comfortable for *both* of you, which means remaining open to accepting and working with each of your comfort zones *and* your respective boundaries. The Platinum Rule does *not* mean you *have* to try anything your mate asks of you, yet it works best if you set and express boundaries from a place of love and compassion, not criticism, judgment, or defensiveness. Try to have fun with this exercise and stay open to learning new insights about yourself and your spouse.

Here are the suggested steps:

1. Begin by getting physically comfortable.
2. Together, agree that you will not have sex with each other or be sexually intimate for the entirety of this exercise.
3. Decide who will go first in the active role. Each of you will have an opportunity to experience being both active and passive as you take turns touching and receiving touch. We suggest choosing a shoulder, hand, or foot massage. We will use a shoulder massage as an example.
4. Begin by touching your partner's shoulders the way you would want to be touched (The Golden Rule).
5. Then, ask for their feedback about what they liked as well as what they didn't like (The Platinum Rule). Feedback may include "go faster" or "go slower," "more pressure" or "less pressure," "focus here, not there," etc.
6. Touch your beloved again, integrating their guidance into your massage.

7. When your mate gives you a thumbs-up, so to speak, switch roles.

8. Take time after massaging each other to discuss your experiences: your spouse's experience being touched, yours being the toucher, and vice versa.

You may discover that your assumptions about how they like to be touched weren't totally accurate. You may also discover new insights about your own preferences.

After testing out this exercise, consider applying The Platinum Rule to your sex life. For those of you who are uncomfortable expressing sexual yearnings verbally, try an alternate approach, such as writing your wishes in a letter or email, or find an online discussion or illustration of what you want and share the URL. There's no one right way to explore The Platinum Rule or express sexual desires and preferences.

# TOOL 16. SKIN-TO-SKIN FOR PARENTS

Many new parents understand the importance of skin-to-skin contact to support bonding with their newborn. However, new parents tend to be much less aware of the importance of fostering a similar secure bond with each other. Skin-to-skin contact powerfully nurtures that adult connection, too.

Before first exploring skin-to-skin time together, set an agreement to not have sex. Doing so removes the pressure to perform or respond in a certain way and allows you to focus on being present in an embodied fashion.

Carve out at least fifteen minutes to get naked with your spouse and spoon or cuddle. Notice the thoughts, emotions, and sensations that arise without trying to fix or change them.

Just notice. If sexual arousal happens, notice that too. Skin-to-skin contact with your beloved often signals safety to your autonomic nervous system and gives you space to begin to relax, let down your guard, and connect nonverbally.

If you both enjoy the experience, schedule another fifteen minutes of skin-to-skin contact in a few days. After these skin-to-skin explorations, schedule a few minutes to discuss what you each liked and didn't like about the experience and adjust accordingly.

Gently inquire of each other: "If you were to add just one micro-step—a small action, a small effort—to increase our connection through this exercise, what would you add?" Come up with three or four small steps and try to agree on one to test out. Schedule that step and see where it leads. Debrief again. If you both decide after trying this out one or more times that you'd like to transition from non-sexual skin-to-skin contact to sexual exploration, go for it!

While Skin-to-Skin for Parents, and the other tools in this section, aren't explicitly—so to speak—about sex, they rekindle your connection with yourself and each other, which provides a path to reignite and deepen your intimacy and the sexual aspect of your relationship together.

CHAPTER 14

In-Laws and Extended Family

While many couples enjoy strong, supportive relationships with in-laws and extended family, new parents sometimes struggle to maintain or establish healthy postpartum boundaries. Common challenges include:

+ Setting realistic expectations about visits, appropriate roles, and advice-giving.
+ Establishing boundaries about what works best for your new family unit.
+ Communicating constructively with family members whose vision of parenting or grandparenting differs from your own.

New parents sometimes struggle to maintain or establish healthy postpartum boundaries.

In many instances, conflict with in-laws and extended family is a matter of personality differences or contrasting parenting styles. In some, hopefully uncommon cases, parents have valid reasons for insisting on supervised visits or cutting off contact altogether, e.g., when physical or emotional safety is at stake.

Negative conflicts with in-laws often cause stress for the parent trying to set boundaries *and* spark torn allegiances for the parent caught in the middle, doing their best to navigate the tension between their beloved and their family of origin. Plus, if one of you came from a family, ethnic, or cultural background in which extended family, including in-laws, were central to childrearing, and one of you grew up with grandparents and extended family members who played a marginal role, those divergent backgrounds can easily collide.

In this chapter, we offer tools to decrease and diffuse conflict for new parents who struggle with in-laws and extended family.

 ## TOOL 17. WHAT'S YOURS IS OURS

This tool is both an attitude and an exercise designed to loosen the hold of drawing lines—at times, battle lines—between what belongs to each of you individually and what belongs to your relationship together. Sometimes the lines are innocuous, e.g., "Hands off *my* favorite mug" or "I'm fine with that hideous Barcalounger as long as you keep it in *your* office." At other times, the stakes are higher, and insisting that what's mine is mine and what's yours is yours not only generates conflict, but it also diminishes trust, caring, and a shared sense of responsibility: "*I* earned this money, so it's *mine* to spend" or "She's *your* mother, so she's *your* problem."

What's Yours Is Ours assumes that, regardless of prior individual ownership, once you commit to being a "we"— especially once *we* have a baby—what was yours and mine is now ours. You *both* share responsibility for it, sometimes equally, sometimes equitably, yet shared, nonetheless.

That's the attitude part: shifting perspective from *mine* or *yours* to *ours*. Here's the exercise part, which puts this shift into action with extended family:

1. If you're the one who has issues with your in-laws or extended family, ask your spouse: "What's important to you about me improving my relationship with your family and adopting more of an '*our* family' approach?"

2. Then ask: "What do you think the positive impact would be on our nuclear family—and our baby—if I shifted my attitude and behavior from 'yours' to 'ours' when it comes to family?"

3. Ask your partner to come up with three to five suggestions for ways you can better share responsibility, such as mending relationships with family members or accepting more invitations to family gatherings.

4. Choose one or two of your spouse's suggestions or try one or two of your own that your mate agrees to. Then, *genuinely* test them out. Being sincere in your efforts is crucial. This isn't about going through the motions of shared responsibility; you need to buy into "what's yours is ours" and act accordingly.

5. Calendar a follow-up conversation in two or three weeks to discuss how things are going and evaluate whether the situation has improved. If so, keep up the good work. If the tactics you tried don't increase co-responsibility, or you find them too challenging to sustain, choose a different approach from your partner's list or your own and then give that one a shot.

 TOOL 18. IN THE WAY OR IN THEIR WAY

This tool shifts negative perceptions of in-laws and extended family from what the Arbinger Institute calls "in the box" thinking—in which you place others in a metaphorical box by treating them as objects or obstacles—to removing the box altogether. Seeing people as obstacles means homing in on how they prevent you from being or doing what you want. When you objectify people, you deny their humanity and treat them as unworthy of your respect and understanding. Either way, you rebuff your in-laws and extended family and see them as *in the way.*

However, if you think of them as people with their own beliefs and behaviors who possess as much right to those beliefs and behaviors as you do to yours, then you honor your shared humanity. You might disagree with them, resent their critical or unsolicited advice, prefer not to spend time with them—or as much time as your spouse desires—*and* you might also find a way to tolerate differences and respond with increased equanimity and acceptance. From this place, you believe that your in-laws are acting or doing things *in their way.*

How can you shift from seeing your partner's family as objects or obstacles to seeing them as people who are different, no better and no worse, than you? Ironically, one option is to think about what you have in common, the ways in which they're like you. For example, while your mother-in-law might have a parenting or baby-care philosophy you oppose, it's likely she loves your baby and wants her to be healthy and happy . . . just like you do.

+ Come up with three to five commonalities you share with your in-laws or your mate's extended family. The first might be that you all love your spouse, and the second might be that you all want what is best for your baby.

+ If you struggle to think of commonalities, approach this from a different angle and ask yourself: "What positive outcomes are they trying to achieve, even if I don't believe they will get there with that approach or I don't like how they want to get there?"

The more you explore what you have in common, the more you imagine the positive outcomes they're trying to achieve, the more you can understand your differences and treat your in-laws and extended family with respect. For example, let's imagine that your mother-in-law wants to give your infant a bottle, yet you're not ready for her to do so and don't like feeling pressured. If you can pause and use empathy to imagine what your mother-in-law may be longing for, you might understand her desire to build a relationship with her grandbaby by bottle-feeding her. Reassuring your mother-in-law that you, too, want them to bond might help lessen the charge, even if your timeline or your strategy to get there differs.

TOOL 19. IDEAL VISION FOR IN-LAWS AND EXTENDED FAMILY

Create a vision of your ideal relationship with your in-laws and extended family, including the roles you'd like them to play in your family's life. One way to do this is to write or audio-record it as a story: Imagine it's twenty years from now and you're reflecting on the wonderful role your in-laws and extended family played in your immediate family's—especially your child(ren)'s—lives.

With that positive perspective in mind, describe what worked well for all of you, how you handled disagreements, how you capably navigated holidays, how your adult child(ren) feels now, twenty years later, about their grandparents and extended family. Create a vision of what worked well.

You can either compose this jointly with your spouse or create separate narratives. If you craft separate visions, once you finish them, share them with each other. Look for commonalities and notice differences. Then explore questions such as:

+ What do you agree on?
+ What are the most important parts of your story?
+ What are the most important parts of your beloved's story according to them?
+ What aspects of their story are you concerned about, and why?
+ What aspects of your story are they concerned about, and why?
+ How can you create a shared vision that honors your respective concerns and what's most important to each of you?

If only one of you creates an ideal vision, review it with your mate and solicit their input. Regardless of how you craft this story or who designs it, once you have a shared vision, come up with two or three micro-steps you can take individually and together to manifest it. For example, you might decide to share all or part of your ideal vision with your in-laws or extended family.

QUICK QUESTIONS

- What's an easy first step toward your ideal relationship with your extended family?
- How can you use this ideal vision for ongoing guidance in your relationship with them?
- How can your ideal vision support a constructive perspective on your extended family if the situation becomes challenging?

~~~~~

PART FOUR

Tools to Connect, Prevent Conflict, De-Escalate, and Repair

~~~~~

In this section, we shift from tools that address the issues that precipitate conflict to tools that enhance the quality and resilience of your relationship. These tools are proactive, reduce the amount and intensity of Fighting Wrong, and help you reconnect after negative conflict.

Here, the focus is on your connection with each other and on finding ways to support, expand, and replenish your capacity to Fight Right and to recover together from Fighting Wrong. Research suggests that doing so is essential, indeed foundational, to long-term relationship satisfaction. In his findings, John Gottman names this key element a "deep friendship," while Sue Johnson's research centers on "nourishing a safe and secure bond." Their common message is the importance of a trusting connection with your spouse. The tools in Part 4 build, enhance, and grow that connection and offer a gateway to Fighting Right.

CHAPTER 15

Tools to Build Connection and Prevent Negative Conflict

The tools in this chapter prioritize maintenance, a concept people assume is necessary for cars, homes, and health, but rarely relationships. Often, we expect relationships to keep functioning well with very little conscious, positive attention or effort. Neglecting relationship maintenance is particularly easy when a new baby arrives, given that parents' alone time with each other decreases significantly. Although a decrease in couple time is inevitable, relationships still need regular care.

> **Often, we expect relationships to keep functioning well with very little conscious, positive attention or effort.**

If you garden, you know it isn't enough to reduce weeds and pests; your garden also needs water, light, and nourishment. Similarly, it isn't sufficient to try to fix or get rid of problems in your relationship without also nourishing your connection.

Improving your bond also helps you Fight Right in multiple ways. When you feel more connected to each other:

+ Fights are less likely to happen in the first place.
+ They resolve more quickly.
+ They rarely reach a destructive intensity.

- ✦ They are taken in stride.
- ✦ They do not disrupt your relationship fulfillment.
- ✦ They do not negatively impact your baby's wellbeing.

The seven tools in this chapter will build the strength and resilience of your friendship and bond.

TOOL 20. GIVE 10 PERCENT

Instead of assuming that your relationship requires a grand gesture for you to reconnect, that you have to give 100 percent effort by, for example, planning an elaborate weekend getaway without your baby, imagine a 10 percent gesture. That might be eating a candlelit dinner on the couch after your baby goes to bed, bringing your stay-at-home partner a cup of tea before you leave for work, or exchanging affectionate texts once a day. Relationship care doesn't have to be a big commitment. What matters most is that you prioritize it, not how much cumulative time you devote to it. As the saying goes: "Small things often."

Small gestures inspire connection, which makes you more likely to try another small gesture, and another. An additional advantage of giving a 10 percent effort is that if it doesn't bring you closer, you're less likely to feel hugely disappointed than if a grand gesture fails. You're also more likely to try out additional small gestures until you find one that works.

TOOL 21. REFLECTIVE AND SPIRITUAL TIME TOGETHER

Spending reflective or spiritual time together, even if for only five minutes a day, helps some parents build a more solid foundation for connection and conflict resolution. Routinizing that practice often provides an opportunity to feel calmer, more centered, and open-hearted with each other. If this kind of practice is important to both of you, it also affirms common values. For some, it taps into something larger—such as a belief in a higher power or a sense of wonder —which offers a unique form of support for your relationship.

Try one or more of these options with your beloved, or come up with your own:

+ Meditate together, such as before going to bed at night or rising in the morning.
+ Pray together at home.
+ Attend a service at a church, synagogue, mosque, Buddhist temple, or another place of faith.
+ Perform a ritual together, e.g., create a gratitude practice, light Sabbath candles, or say grace before meals.
+ Chant, sing, dance, or play music together.

 ## TOOL 22. BELLY-TO-BELLY HUG

Drawn from the work of Dr. Stan Tatkin, author of *Wired for Love*, these steps help you and your partner physically connect, relax, and create a shared sense of safety:

1. Without words, hug each other belly to belly until you feel your own and your spouse's bodies relax.
2. Tune in to your breath, gently and calmly belly breathe together, and release into your embrace more fully.
3. After you both relax into each other, hold your hug for whatever time frame feels comfortable and then slowly let go.

This nonverbal exercise "speaks" directly to and soothes your flight, fight, freeze, or appease reactivity and allows you to connect to your mate on an instinctive level. Your "animal" bodies feel safer and calmer when connected. By holding each other belly to belly and relaxing into each other's breath, warmth, bodies, and heartbeat—even by smelling each other's scent—you co-soothe together.

This simple activity helps settle your autonomic nervous systems and creates emotional and physiological attunement. This tool may be especially important and reassuring when sexual intimacy is decreased.

Because the transition from day to evening can set the tone for the rest of your waking time together, the belly-to-belly hug is particularly useful as a homecoming exercise, especially when prioritized as the first thing that happens when a returning partner enters the house. Before talking to each other, greeting pets, dealing with chores, or cuddling the baby, reestablish your nonverbal connection with this hug. This reactivates your bond and helps you better navigate challenges as a team.

 ## TOOL 23. CHECK IN AND SCALE

Make a regular habit—perhaps at the same time once a week—to check in with your spouse. Here are a few useful questions to ask each other:

+ What are you grateful for?
+ What are you finding challenging?
+ What's in the way of you feeling clear and loving with each other?[5]
+ What could you do that would help you both feel more like a team?

+ What does your relationship need to be as healthy and alive as possible?

In addition to asking these questions, consider scaling how you feel individually and in your relationship. On a ten-point scale, with one being "terrible" and ten "amazing," rate how you feel individually and then rate how you feel in your relationship in that moment. For example, "Today, I'm at a five for myself and an eight in our relation-ship." Then invite your partner to scale as well. To deepen your understanding of each other's scores and turn them into opportunities for connection, explore these Quick Questions.

> *What could you do that would help you both feel more like a team?*

QUICK QUESTIONS

- What's happening right now that contributes to your individual number?
- Ask your spouse: What's one small thing I can do to improve your number, even if only half a point?
- What's one small thing you can do to improve that number for yourself?
- What's going on right now that's contributing to the number you scaled for our relationship?
- Ask your spouse: What's one small thing I can do to improve that relationship number, even if only half a point?
- What's one small thing you can do to improve your relationship number?

TOOL 24. THE STORY OF US

This tool encourages you to nurture your bond by creating your relationship story. This can be achieved verbally, in writing, or through other creative means: drawing a picture, singing, making a collage, choreographing a dance, or playing a song. The intent is to revisit the positive experiences and emotions that brought you together and share what first attracted you and what you most enjoyed about each other in the early stages of your relationship.

You can also tap into The Story of Us with a quick remark: "I remember how much you made me laugh on our first date"—or by proposing a shared activity: "Let's look at our wedding photos after the baby goes to sleep."

TOOL 25. CULTIVATE COMPASSION

As simple as it sounds, compassionate communication—regardless of whether the topic is mundane or fraught—enhances closeness and curtails negative conflict. It isn't always easy to summon up compassion, especially because new parenthood and sleep deprivation increase the likelihood of feeling irritable, insecure, or critical. The good news is that just intending to be compassionate often opens your heart, even if only a little.

The root of the word "compassion" means "to suffer with" and connotes a desire to relieve another's suffering. Compassion is intimately connected to empathy, the ability to sense and share other people's emotions, coupled with the ability to imagine what they might be thinking or feeling.

At times, you may need to acknowledge to yourself: "Okay, I notice that part of me is feeling critical, *and* I know in the big picture, my intention is to be compassionate." If feeling hurt or unsupported interferes with your ability to express compassion, remind yourself that your partner feels vulnerable too.

How can you practice compassion? Here are three ways:

+ Imagine putting yourself in your spouse's shoes and, for fun, try on their *actual* shoes—even if you can only squeeze your toes in—and see what that experience offers.
+ When you feel triggered by your partner's behavior, words, or attitude, ask yourself: "What would the compassionate part of me say?" If you ask this question initially about minor differences, you'll be better prepared to apply it when life gets challenging so you can nip negative conflict in the bud.
+ Even if you disagree, first, get curious about your spouse's perspective and, second, allow for the possibility that their experience, while different from your own, remains valid. As Dr. Brené Brown notes in a popular meme: "In order to empathize with someone's experience, you must be willing to believe them as they see it and not as how you imagine their experience to be." *And* not as how you want it to be or think it should be.

TOOL 26. RECOGNIZE EACH OTHER'S EFFORTS TO CONNECT

Recognizing and responding to each other's efforts to connect is a practical way to feel closer on a daily basis. When sleep deprivation and other parenting demands intervene, it's that much harder to notice your beloved's quick peck on the cheek, the cup of coffee he placed next to you when you were breast-feeding, or the silly joke they cracked when the baby started crying as soon as you started to nap. Yet responding to these efforts deepens your bond. Plus, while each effort may seem like a small thing, even small gestures can make a big difference.

Honing your awareness and skill in *recognizing* your spouse's connective efforts can warm up your interactions and enhance relationship satisfaction. Research suggests that couples with the highest levels of relationship fulfillment recognize each other's efforts to connect about 85 percent of the time, while those with very low relationship satisfaction do so about a third of the time. Yet even under ideal circumstances, you sometimes miss your mate's efforts. As Dr. Sue Johnson, founder of Emotionally Focused Therapy, notes: "We all send unclear signals and misread cues. We become distracted, we suddenly shift our level of emotional intensity and leave our partner behind, or we simply overload each other with too many signals and messages." In other words, it's normal to send signals that get missed, or miss signals that get sent.

The first step in recognizing each other's connection bids is to increase awareness of your own by asking ourselves, "How do I try to connect with my mate?" and thinking about the efforts we initiate, such as touch, compliments, humor, and eye contact. Given different preferences and personalities, failed connection attempts—while painful—provide an opportunity to get to know each other better and get more intentional about deepening your bond. So, once you identify how you try to connect, consider testing the following dialogue. Remember to speak to each other kindly and respectfully and switch roles so you can learn about both of your connection bids.

Here are the steps in the conversation:

1. **Spouse #1:** "How do you think I try to connect with you?"

2. **Spouse #2:** Offer *at least* three responses. Then ask, "What did I miss?"

3. **Spouse #1:** List connection bids they missed, if any.

4. **Spouse #2:** "How would you like me to respond to your efforts to connect?"

5. **Spouse #1:** Let your partner know your preferred response(s). For example, "Smile at me," "Turn toward me physically," "Reach out and gently touch me," or "Say something in response."

6. **Spouse #2:** If you're willing to do so, and your partner requests it, take time to increase your awareness of and responsiveness to your beloved's efforts to connect, even if only by a small percentage. If you feel uneasy with or really dislike the kind of connection your partner offers, let them know that approach doesn't work for you and ask if it would be okay to ramp up your responsiveness to a different one.

7. **Spouse #1:** Respond as kindly as possible if your mate struggles to connect in ways that you prefer. As we've explored elsewhere in this book, differences abound in relationships, including in what brings you closer.

Feel free to revise those steps to better fit your priorities, yet make sure you switch roles so you both get a chance to ask and answer questions. However you choose to recognize each other's attempts to connect, remember that perfection isn't the goal. Your objective is an enhanced and deeper bond.

 ## TOOL 27. HONOR YOUR TRANSITION TO PARENTHOOD

Whether you become a parent by giving birth, partnering with someone who gives birth, fostering, adopting, or surrogacy, all parents experience a more or less abrupt shift from one state of existence—childlessness—to a new state of being: parenthood.

> **All parents experience a more or less abrupt shift from childlessness to a new state of being: parenthood.**

That change is both tangible (one day you don't have kids, and the next day you do) and intangible (becoming a parent involves internal shifts in identity and in how you prioritize tasks and decisions, relate to your spouse, and approach life in general). William Bridges describes this as the difference between change, which is situational and tangible, and transition, which is emotional and psychological. He describes transition as "the inner reorientation and self-redefinition that you have to go through in order to incorporate . . . changes into your life."

According to Bridges, most of life's changes, including parenthood, are disruptive both internally and in your relationship with others. Successful change depends on recognizing that in order to thrive in your new role and new chapter of life, a familiar and, perhaps, cherished chapter and role must end. All transitions include losses and gains. Some new parents report a disconnect, time lag, or other adjustment between the arrival of a baby and fully embracing their role as a parent.

Examples of an uneven transition from what-was to what-is include: Your spouse laments their sudden loss of independence and bridles against their new parenting responsibilities; they complain bitterly that sexual spontaneity is gone; or perhaps they panic and declare that parenthood was a mistake! Instead of criticizing them, presuming their immaturity, ignoring their complaints, or assuming they don't love your baby as much as you do, try to give them—and perhaps you, too—space to articulate and accept the losses, endings, and adjustments inherent in becoming parents.

Admitting that you miss aspects of, and feel grief for, the life you left behind is *not* the same as rejecting your baby or your new role as a parent. Instead, it may be a form of constructive venting and a way to honor this rite of passage as one chapter ends and a new one begins.

QUICK QUESTIONS

- What aspects of life without children will you miss the most?
- What parts of your relationship do you most want to hold on to?
- What will most help you let go of the past and step more fully into your new present?
- How might parenthood grow who you are and enhance your relationship?

CHAPTER 16

Tools to De-Escalate When You Fight Wrong

Most parents recognize, or learn to recognize, when a slow-burning argument is about to explode into a wildfire. Noticing your own and your partner's physiological and interpersonal "tells"—behavioral or emotional signals that the intensity of your disagreement is about to shift dramatically—allows you to change course, take a break and regroup, or calm down enough to communicate constructively rather than throw gasoline on the fire. Tools 28–31 can help that process.

 ## TOOL 28. KNOW YOUR TRIGGERS

Knowing your triggers prevents unnecessary relationship damage through self-awareness. In the aftermath of a fight, it's common to recognize that your reaction was out of proportion to what happened. You ask yourself: "Why did I get so mad at that relatively minor thing? I went from zero to sixty so fast!" Or: "What just happened to make me clam up and shut down during that conversation?" These kinds of responses to conflict are referred to as getting triggered, activated, or dysregulated. This occurs when a topic, event, or some other stimulus touches old wounds, familiar fears, or traumas. Triggers include other people's behaviors, phrases, words, tone of voice, body language, facial expressions, and emotions, as well as subject matter, environments, circumstances, and other kinds of sensory input like sounds, tastes, or smells.

It takes intention and self-awareness to learn what sets you off. Armed with that information, you are in a much better position to prevent triggered reactions and the negative conflicts that sometimes result.

+ In thinking about past conflicts, whether with your spouse, an ex, or your family of origin, what do you consider to be your most familiar and recurrent triggers?
+ If you struggle to recognize your main triggers, consider asking your beloved, a trusted friend, or a close family member for input. Over time, those closest to you often notice the factors or circumstances that most contribute to your reactivity.

Also, knowing your triggers and their impact helps you take responsibility for your reactions, which is key to reducing unproductive conflict. For example, if you had a critical father, you may intervene quickly, protectively, and harshly if your spouse expresses feelings of irritation or impatience with you or the baby. Yet if this wasn't already a charged issue for you, you might respond with greater tolerance, curiosity, or compassion.

Parenting commonly surfaces unrecognized or unresolved childhood issues. You may get activated more than usual. Although uncomfortable, your reactions are like arrows pointing the way toward parts of yourself that need attention and healing. If significant trauma contributes to your triggers, we encourage you to seek professional assistance.

Knowing your triggers is a prerequisite to managing their impact on you and others. One of the best ways to begin that self-management effort is to use neutral or compassionate self-talk to name or acknowledge being activated. You might say to yourself: "I'm noticing that I'm triggered. Time to slow down." Or lean into self-compassion and note: "I feel really reactive, and that's okay. I'll be all right. Let me take a breath."

> *Knowing your triggers and their impact helps you take responsibility for your reactions, which is key to reducing unproductive conflict.*

Telling your partner that you're activated is a helpful next step. Once you self-regulate, consider sharing your triggers with them and, if possible, describe the original source of your reactivity or what you suspect it is if you're unsure. Sharing helps your mate understand you better and not take your reactive responses so personally.

Recognizing the early signs of reactivity and taking a break before it escalates, or intervening as soon as possible when it does, is an important skill that takes time and ongoing practice.

TOOL 29. DEAL WITH FLOODING

Flooding refers to a physiological state of overwhelm that occurs when you feel threatened and stress hormones surge in your body. Common symptoms of flooding include shallow, rapid breathing; heart palpitations; muscular tension such as a clenched jaw, tightness in your shoulders, chest, or throat;

feeling overheated; increased perspiration; lightheadedness; or stomach discomfort. Flooding not only impairs your ability to activate executive functioning in your brain and nervous system, i.e., empathy, logic, planning, and thoughtful word choice, but it also limits your ability to listen to and converse with others.

Noticing, and sharing with your spouse, when your nervous system is too revved up for constructive communication is invaluable. This simple tool helps you recognize your own and your partner's signs of flooding, which signal activation of fight, flight, freeze, or fawn reactions. Because some people are more prone to flooding than others, identifying that tendency in yourself and your spouse not only enhances your understanding of each other, but it also inspires compassion.

Here are suggested steps to help you notice and respond to flooding. Feel free to pick and choose which ones to explore or try them all out:

- Pause at the first sign of escalating conflict and pay attention to what's happening in your body.
- Make a mental note of tense or tight areas and other symptoms of physiological unease or stress. The more you practice noticing how you feel, the better you can track early physiological changes in your nervous system. Doing so lessens the intensity of those changes.
- Share what you discovered with your partner. Why? So, if they notice changes in you during disagreements in the future, they can ask: "How's your throat feeling right now?" or "What's happening in your body?" or "How about we take a break?"
- If you discover that one or both of you floods, create a strategy to help during conflict, such as an

agreed-upon hand signal to let your spouse know you are flooding. Upon seeing that signal, your beloved's job is to stop talking and delay the conversation until you self-regulate.

+ If you decide to take a break, be sure to schedule a time to check back in and assess if you're ready to continue the conversation. Make good use of the break to settle your nervous system by taking a walk, journaling, or doing a breathing exercise.*

Once you understand your flooding responses, you can learn ways to prevent or limit them and soothe yourself when flooding occurs.

If you discover that your spouse floods easily, do your best to respond with compassion instead of frustration. Getting angry with someone for a reaction they can't control only increases the problem. Offer your understanding and suggest a break so everyone can calm down.

QUICK QUESTIONS

- How might communication with your mate improve if you acknowledge feeling flooded?

- How might communication improve if you understand that your partner sometimes (or often) floods when you fight?

- How does your body let you know you are flooding?

---

* For more information on self-regulating, see Tool 30, Practice Self-Soothing, and Tool 31, Taking Time Tool.

 TOOL 30. PRACTICE SELF-SOOTHING

New parents often recognize the importance of babies learning to self-soothe and want to help their little ones develop this critical, lifelong skill. By "self-soothing," we mean the ability to move through distress and regain equilibrium. Unfortunately, many parents cannot reliably count on their *own* ability to self-soothe because they didn't learn adequate self-regulating skills in infancy and childhood. If you struggle to calm yourself when upset, you are not alone.

Since so much parenting involves modeling desirable behaviors, responses, and attitudes for children, it's essential that you learn how to calm yourself. Doing so is an integral skill for daily living that helps you feel more serene and centered as a parent, partner, and human. Stated simply, you need to be good at calming yourself when things get tense to avoid reacting in ways that make things worse.

> *Since so much parenting involves modeling desirable behaviors, responses, and attitudes for children, it's essential that you learn how to calm yourself.*

Plus, research shows that states of autonomic arousal—feeling flooded, emotionally reactive, or triggered—are contagious; your stress directly influences your spouse's and baby's moods, and vice versa.

When your nervous system revs up, you have many options for reversing the process and settling down. What constitutes successful self-soothing is unique to each individual, but the classic place to start is with your breath. Breathing is powerful because it can be automatically *or* consciously controlled, thus linking your central and autonomic nervous systems. When you feel threatened, your heartbeat quickens and your breathing becomes shallower, often without your awareness.

Any of these tips can make a big difference:

+ Take three slow, relaxed, deep belly-breaths before you speak or react.
+ When you inhale, count beats in your head. As you release your breath, add two or three beats to your exhale. Repeat five times.
+ Place one hand gently on your chest and the other on your belly. Hold this position for five to ten beats as you breathe at a normal pace.
+ Count slowly to five inside your head before responding.
+ Tune into your body. Notice the soles of your feet touching the floor, how your belly rises and falls with each breath, and the position of your arms.
+ Move your body in a way that releases tension. Wiggle your fingers, shrug your shoulders, stretch your arms, unclench your jaw, and roll your neck.
+ Take a short walk, focus your attention on each step you take, and count your steps until you feel yourself relax more.

TOOL 31. TAKING TIME TOOL

Drawn from the Toolbox Project®, a research-based K–6 Social Emotional Learning program developed by family therapist Mark Collin, the Taking Time Tool offers a two-part way to de-escalate.[6] The first component—"time in"—involves shifting your focus from what's occurring outside of you to self-awareness. This might include checking in with yourself to acknowledge that you feel triggered, naming the emotions coming up, noticing the tense parts of your body, or focusing on your breath to reconnect with your physical and internal experience.

The second component—"time away"—means literally walking away from a situation or person you find triggering so you can regroup. It is essential to let your partner know, in the moment, that you are leaving to soothe yourself and that you will be back. While opinions vary on exactly how much time to take before returning to your conversation, we suggest a *minimum* of twenty minutes and a maximum of twenty-four hours. If one or both of you still feels flooded, add more time as needed.

In contrast to a time-out, which has a punitive connotation, the Taking Time Tool offers a gentle, self-regulating, and self-caring way to intervene when a negative situation escalates. When this tool is used in a classroom setting, children are encouraged to rejoin the group when they feel calmer. The same holds true for you and your beloved. Once you lower your internal intensity around an issue or interaction, reconvene and address the topic directly, with calmness guiding your words and actions.

In some instances, you might ultimately choose to skip discussing the issue because, after taking time in and time away, you realize the problem isn't really a relationship problem and is tied instead to your own triggers, memories, mood, or assumptions. If that occurs, please share those insights with your mate so they better understand your preference to let things go. If they, too, believe the issue is minor and unworthy of further consideration, drop it. However, if they want to chat about what occurred, try to be open to that request.

CHAPTER 17

Tools To Repair

Since conflict is inevitable and no one engages in it perfectly all the time, knowing how to repair or "kiss and make up" is essential, though the saying might be more helpful if it were "make up and kiss." Tools in this section are designed to soften and mend small and large emotional injuries caused by Fighting Wrong.

 ## TOOL 32. REPAIR STRATEGIES

Couples need ways to heal the damage from unskilled fights, while staying open to each other's attempts to restore the connection. Making *and* receiving repair efforts are different yet interrelated skills essential to recovering from Fighting Wrong.

Spend a few minutes together when you're *not* fighting to come up with a list of repair strategies that work for you, including words or phrases you are open to hearing from your partner that would calm your distress, as well as nonverbal

> **Couples need ways to heal the damage from unskilled fights, while staying open to each other's attempts to restore the connection.**

repair cues. Allow for individual differences as much as possible, e.g., one of you might yearn to be touched after you fight, while being touched too soon deepens wounds for the other.

While you are probably aware of your own attempts to make up with your spouse, noticing their repair strategies might require more intentional effort and openness. Which, if any, of these examples of verbal and nonverbal repair do you recognize in you or your partner? Which ones would you like to cultivate?

+ Apologize: Make it specific and sincere, and don't undermine your apology by inserting the word "but."
+ Say words like: "I messed up," "I didn't mean to upset you," or "We'll get through this."
+ Offer a tender, conciliatory touch.
+ Joke to lighten the mood.
+ Give a thoughtful gift.
+ Smile at your spouse.
+ Assist with or complete a task, especially an unpleasant one.

At times, it is difficult to accept or respond warmly to your mate's repair efforts. You may simply not be ready yet. If so, we suggest you try to acknowledge their attempt to reconnect and let them know you need more time or discussion.

QUICK QUESTIONS

• When you have a bad fight, what are two or three things your partner could do or say to help repair the damage?

- Ask your spouse: If we have a bad fight, what are two or three things I can do or say afterward to help mend the rift between us?
- What attitudes and intentions help you open up to your partner's repair efforts?

TOOL 33. PIVOT

This term comes from basketball, where it refers to keeping one foot in place while moving the other one. Here, the idea is to shift from your current position—the one that likely hurt your spouse—to a new one. For example, if you just told your beloved what they're doing wrong, pivot to what they're doing right.

Pivoting can happen by degrees; you can still maintain your own beliefs while simultaneously naming aspects of your beloved's perspective that you understand or, perhaps, agree with. Let's consider two new dads who disagree on the topic of babysitting. One believes their baby is too young to be left alone with anyone other than her dads or their immediate family, all of whom live far away. The other dad wants a date night to help them reconnect and thinks it's okay for them to hire a highly recommended and experienced sitter for a few hours. The dad who resists a babysitter might pivot toward his partner by acknowledging how nice it would be to have more time alone as a couple or that he fondly remembers the days when they could spontaneously go out to eat. The other dad might pivot by acknowledging how scary it is to leave their baby alone and how much he appreciates his spouse's concern for their child's safety and wellbeing. None of those comments diminishes either parent's perspective, yet they offer a small pivot, maybe 10 or 15 degrees, toward each other.

A 30-degree pivot might mean finding a part of your partner's perspective that you align with or some aspect of your own position you agree to compromise. For example, "I understand that you don't want to offend your parents, and I'm willing to find a way to include them, but I really don't want them staying with us for that whole week."

An example of a 180-degree pivot would be owning up to that moment in an argument when you realize you are wrong! Isn't that an awful feeling? Maybe you are self-righteously defending your position that it's your spouse's turn to get up with the baby when something clicks in your brain: "Oops, I didn't get up last night. That was the night before!" It takes maturity to pause, take a breath, and say: "I just realized I'm wrong about that. Sorry!"

QUICK QUESTIONS

- What gets in the way of your willingness to pivot?
- How might pivoting help you better resolve one of your areas of negative conflict?
- If you were to shift just 10 or 20 degrees from an entrenched position on one of your disagreements, what would you say or do?

 TOOL 34. PARTS OF ME LANGUAGE

As human beings, it's a normal and common experience to feel more than one emotion at any given time or have competing thoughts or beliefs. Although this can be confusing and complicated, it's also part of the richness and paradox of life.

During conflict, often one part of you wants to win or be right, while another part wants to reconnect with your partner and find a constructive resolution. By naming various parts of your experience, you create space to move forward in a way that holds both your complexity and your integrity.

> **During conflict, often one part of you wants to win or be right, while another part wants to reconnect with your partner and find a constructive resolution.**

The first step in this process involves recognizing the presence of more than one feeling, emotion, impulse, belief, thought, or need. Then, by sharing those parts with your spouse, you provide an opportunity for constructive communication and, likely, reduce your own and your mate's reactivity. If you prefer, try the phrase "something in me" instead of "part of me;" you might find "something in me" softer and less definitive.

Here are a few examples:

+ "Part of me feels stubborn and wants to win this fight and prove you wrong, and part of me just wants to kiss and make up."

+ "One part of me wants to trust that you mean what you're saying, another part is afraid of getting hurt again, and another part is too tired to deal with any of this!"
+ "Something in me is so hurt and mad at you, while something else in me understands your perspective, or at least part of it."

Some of these examples involve a willingness to get beneath angry and critical reactions and name a part of you that also feels hurt, rejected, or scared. This tool invites courage to be less attacking or defensive, and more open and vulnerable.

The benefits of acknowledging the complexity of your emotional reactions to your partner extend well beyond your relationship. They include modeling and teaching your child Emotional Intelligence (EQ), expanding your vocabulary for self-expression, and deepening self-knowledge.

QUICK QUESTIONS

- What would help you find the courage to share a more vulnerable part of yourself with your partner instead of just voicing the reactive or entrenched parts?
- How might giving voice to a less blaming and confrontational part of you help ease or avoid a power struggle with your mate?
- What are some of the different parts of you that you felt the last time you argued?

TOOL 35. THE POWER OF FORGIVENESS

The ability and willingness to forgive your spouse after a hurtful experience is a powerful expression of love and trust that can deepen intimacy. Mindfulness teacher Jack Kornfield says: "We forgive not to condone, not to say . . . [the wrongdoing] was fine, but to let go of false illusions that we can change the past." Forgiveness is, then, not only a gift to your partner but also a gift to you. It frees you up from carrying the load of a grudge or resentment over time.

Please remember that forgiving differs from forgetting in important ways: You can forgive and still remember what that person did or said that hurt or otherwise upset you. You can forgive and maintain appropriate boundaries for self-protection, if needed. Sometimes you think you've forgiven, yet resentment reemerges over time, perhaps triggered by a new interaction or a memory. This is a normal part of the process.

Why prioritize forgiveness in your relationship? Because it supports connection and repair and prevents the accumulation of unresolved "baggage." It also allows you to get unstuck from the past and, together, experience the challenges and wonders of the present. That being said, the path to forgiveness isn't always straight or simple.

- ✦ Sometimes forgiveness depends on feeling understood or better understanding each other.
  - ✦ What do you want your spouse to better understand about how they hurt you? How can you better understand what motivated their behavior?

- ✦ Sometimes you withhold forgiveness because it feels too vulnerable, especially if you believe your partner might interpret it as a license to hurt you again.
  - ✦ How can you convey to your spouse that forgiving and forgetting are separate for you?
  - ✦ What can your beloved say to reassure you?

Forgiveness is a process that cannot be forced, yet simply holding the desire and intention to forgive is powerful and can help you keep moving in that direction.

Just as you or your spouse may apologize or repair without words, e.g., by helping with a task or offering a gentle touch, so, too, can forgiveness be conveyed nonverbally with a smile, a loving gesture, or a kind tone of voice.

If you continue to worry that forgiving means condoning or forgetting past wrongs, including persistent hurtful patterns, then use "part of me" or equivocating language to forgive, to remember, to set a boundary, or to make a request. For example, you might say: "One part of me forgives you for yelling at me yesterday, while another part remembers the sting of your angry words," or "I forgive you for [fill in the blank] and believe it's part of a negative pattern in our relationship that I want us to address." In both instances, you pardon your partner while simultaneously honoring your past experience with them. As the second statement suggests, forgiving and proactively trying to change your relationship for the better can coexist.

PART FIVE

Troubleshooting

As we near the end of *Fight Right for Your Baby*, we turn our attention to insights into extenuating factors that exacerbate Fighting Wrong, some of which are tied to new parenthood, such as traumatic birth experiences, and some of which are not, such as addiction. Our intent is to name and normalize those struggles *and*, in some instances, suggest additional support beyond what a book can offer.

In this section, we also normalize what most people in long-term relationships know: Many of the issues you fight about are perpetual. Like horror movie monsters, they reanimate over and over again no matter how hard you try to put them to rest. Learning to accept and capably accommodate recurrent, enduring disagreements is in and of itself a path to Fighting Right. Another noteworthy aspect of Fighting Right explored in this part of the book is to differentiate letting go of conflict from avoiding it. While conflict avoidance sometimes seems like a positive strategy, it often increases Fighting Wrong by sending negativity underground, where it festers and expands. Bottom line: Whether in collaboration with your beloved or by studying tools on your own, growing your Fight Right skill set increases your individual, relationship, and familial wellbeing.

CHAPTER 18

You Keep Fighting about the Same Issues Over and Over Again

Although it might sound like bad news, understanding and accepting that all relationships have unsolvable problems can help you take them less personally and address them collaboratively. As couples therapist Dan Wile says, "Every couple has its own set of unsolvable problems that they grapple with throughout the relationship. Creating a platform—operating as joint troubleshooters—is the premier way to deal with such problems."

For example, you might want your mate to be more (or perhaps less) social, or affectionate, or athletic, or communicative, or [fill in the blank], yet they will never become what you yearn for—at least not to the degree you want—because that's not who they are or what they desire. Feeling some degree of disappointment in your spouse is inevitable and a normal part of relationships. No one person can ever fully meet all your needs and desires.

Feeling some degree of disappointment in your spouse is inevitable and a normal part of relationships.

When you look at conflict from this perspective, it becomes easier to let go of polarizing right-wrong, win-lose frameworks and not take your disagreements so personally.[†]

QUICK QUESTIONS

- What are some of your unsolvable problems, the issues that recur in your relationship?
- How might it assist your relationship if you accepted that most, if not all, of those issues will remain unresolved?
- What might it look like to move forward together despite perpetual issues?

While many relationship challenges cannot be fully and finally resolved, they *can* be managed if you're willing to communicate about them. Tools 36 and 37 can help you and your partner navigate unsolvable problems more skillfully.

TOOL 36. NAME THE PROBLEM

Sometimes you get so used to your chronic issues that you're midway into a familiar argument before you realize that you've been here many times before! When both of you know your own and your spouse's lines by heart, try a different approach. A great way to better manage these moments is to name the issues or the parts you play in familiar arguments. Try coming up with silly or fun monikers to make it easier to laugh at the problem or lighten the mood.

---

† See Tool 37, Reframe Chronic Issues, for more guidance.

For example, if money is one of your perpetual issues and you're keener to save than your partner, perhaps you can lighten the mood by declaring: "I'm being Tom Tightwad again!" Please limit name-calling to yourself; it's okay to dub yourself "Tom Tightwad," yet unwise to call your spouse "Spending Sally," unless she likes that name! Also, as tempting as it might be, refrain from using your in-laws' or extended family members' names.

Another option is for you to bestow a title on your familiar argument and announce something like: "We're going down the Money Madness Road." Or simply comment: "I think we've had this fight before. What can we do differently this time?"

Naming the problem allows you to take a step back and witness what is happening instead of getting caught up in it. Naming can prevent you from identifying with, and getting stuck in, your familiar role in the pattern. It helps to slow things down, which is always a good idea with unproductive conflict. Try to remind each other that all relationships have unsolvable issues and drop the subject, agree to disagree, or find a productive way to deal with the problem in the moment, even if it remains unresolved in the long run.

TOOL 37. REFRAME CHRONIC ISSUES

Reframing means shifting your perspective on persistent issues instead of trying to solve a perpetual problem or convince each other of who's right or wrong. One reframing technique is to accept that your fundamental differences mean you're dealing with the equivalent of a chronic health issue, like migraine headaches. You might wish you didn't get them, resent them at times, pretend they don't exist, or forget about them . . . until you get a migraine again. In other words, as enticing as those approaches sound, none cures your headaches.

If you approach your unsolvable issues like migraines, you can turn your attention to effective strategies to live with them.

Here are a few questions to help you and your partner do so:

- ✦ How can you avoid the triggers of your perpetual issue?
- ✦ If you feel a perpetual issue coming on, how can you relieve the discomfort and lower its intensity as quickly and effectively as possible?
- ✦ If you do or say something that triggers a perpetual issue, how can you minimize your own and your beloved's suffering?
- ✦ What preventive measures will help reduce the frequency or severity of the perpetual issue?
- ✦ If the perpetual issue triggers a full-blown fight, how can you alleviate the negative fallout and recover as quickly as possible?

By applying these questions to persistent relationship challenges, you limit your own reactivity, communicate more positively and effectively, and avoid getting stuck in repetitive, negative arguments.

CHAPTER 19

Your Spouse Won't Read This Book: What Should You Do?

Ideally, you will read this book together—or in tandem—and test out exercises as a team. Yet one fact that gets thrown into high relief when you have a baby is that you don't always agree with each other, which includes not always agreeing on what might help you Fight Right or whether you need to learn to Fight Right at all. That's the bad news.

Even if only one of you learns how to repair or constructively address disagreements, your efforts can positively impact your relationship.

The good news is that even if only one of you learns how to repair or constructively address disagreements, your efforts can positively impact your relationship. Who knows? Maybe your spouse will be so impressed with how you now approach conflict that they will read it, too.

Some tools can be more easily practiced solo than others. Here are some tools to try on your own:

+ Tool 2   Money Types
+ Tool 8   Share the Story
+ Tool 9   What's Important to You about That?

- ✦ Tool 13 Self-Nurturing Alone Time
- ✦ Tool 14 Get Rid of Your Buts . . . Right Now
- ✦ Tool 18 In the Way or in Their Way
- ✦ Tool 25 Cultivate Compassion
- ✦ Tool 27 Honor Your Transition to Parenthood
- ✦ Tool 28 Know Your Triggers
- ✦ Tool 29 Deal with Flooding
- ✦ Tool 30 Practice Self-Soothing
- ✦ Tool 33 Pivot
- ✦ Tool 34 Parts of Me Language
- ✦ Tool 35 The Power of Forgiveness
- ✦ Tool 38 Diffuse Parental Shame
- ✦ Tool 39 Get to Know Your Saboteurs
- ✦ Tool 42 Values Exploration

Relationships are like the mobiles new parents often hang above their baby's crib: When one piece of the mobile moves—when one person shifts—everything adjusts in response. While there are no guarantees about whether those adjustments will turn out the way you want, you may be pleasantly surprised. For example, if you start using the Parts of Me Tool, your partner might respond in kind and mirror your softer, more inclusive language. They might notice that the tool de-escalates the charge of what you're expressing and creates more space for them to move toward you.

CHAPTER 20

You Don't Fight.
You Don't Connect Either.

While low levels of relationship conflict can be good, that's not always the case. True, many small battles are not worth fighting about *if* you let them go and move on without resentment. Choose your battles based on whether or not you're able to do that.

If avoiding conflict is a dominant strategy in your relationship, it comes with a price: It creates distance and toxic undercurrents. In the short run, you may gain a certain kind of peace but at the cost of intimacy and connection. If you notice a flatness or lack of aliveness with each other, conflict avoidance may be the culprit. Try to be compassionate with yourself and your spouse if either or both of you tend to avoid conflict.

> **If avoiding conflict is a dominant strategy in your relationship, it comes with a price.**

One couple discovered their avoidant tendencies when they learned about the four primary toxic communication styles—contempt, criticism, defensiveness, and stonewalling—and realized they both shut down around conflict. Before comprehending that they stonewall, they took pride in how little they fought and assumed all was good in their relationship.

Once they named their conflict avoidance, they began to recognize the fallout from this pattern, which included an erosion of self-trust and trust in each other, and a feeling of increasing distance between them. As expecting parents keen on welcoming their baby into as healthy an environment as possible, they slowly but surely increased their tolerance for conflict by gently bringing up disagreements and talking them through.

Often, conflict avoidance is a behavior learned from role models in your family of origin or results from painful or traumatic experiences that included destructive fighting or rejection. As a result, shifting this pattern may stir up painful or difficult feelings, such as fear, resistance, sadness, or anger. Take one small step at a time to build tolerance for and, eventually, comfort with Fighting Right.

Here are five steps to shift from conflict avoidance that undermines your relationship to conflict resolution that brings you closer:

1. Acknowledge the pattern: e.g., "I notice that a lot of our issues are not getting worked out because we avoid conflict."
2. Name the cost to your relationship: e.g., "I think this pattern is causing a buildup of resentment and distance between us."
3. Set an intention: e.g., "I want us to get more comfortable and build trust in our ability to deal with conflict honestly and productively."
4. Start with something small: e.g., a minor issue you've been avoiding.
5. Use one of the Fight Right tools in this book to address the issue.

CHAPTER 21

Complicating Factors

While having a baby puts stress on all relationships, a range of factors increases new parenting challenges and, therefore, increases your risk of Fighting Wrong. These situations benefit from mutual understanding and, sometimes, warrant special attention and assistance. Do one or more of these complicating factors apply to you, your spouse, or your family?

Postpartum Mood Disorders

Almost all those who give birth find the postpartum period challenging, at least at times. Most experience a fairly brief, normal period of increased emotional lability, often called "Baby Blues," which usually passes on its own within the first six weeks after birth.

Of greater concern is that between 15 to 20 percent of those who give birth experience a persistent clinical level of depression, anxiety, or OCD (obsessive-compulsive disorder) symptoms during the first postpartum year. This impacts their relationship with their partners and babies. Moms need help recovering from postpartum mood disorders, which may include joining a support group, starting medication, and/or attending psychotherapy.

Recent research reveals that vulnerability to postpartum mood disorders might be even more acute for lesbians and bisexual mothers than heterosexual ones, and that new fathers, too, are at risk for depression.[7] Relationships in which one or more spouse experiences a mood disorder may benefit from counseling together, separately, or both.

Postpartum psychosis is a far rarer condition—one or two in every thousand—in which a new parent loses touch with reality and may experience severe agitation, delusions, or hallucinations. This condition requires immediate professional intervention because judgment can be quite impaired, and the person may be a danger to themselves or others.

Difficult and Traumatic Birth Experiences

A traumatic birth experience is one that overwhelms a birthing parent's ability to stay present and cope and causes a fight, flight, or freeze response in their autonomic nervous system. Fathers and other non-birthing partners, too, are often impacted by what they witness during difficult births.

It is hard to know how many people experience mild to full-blown post-traumatic symptoms after childbirth because of varying definitions and criteria and because this kind of distress is often trivialized and dismissed by healthcare professionals. According to Penny Simkin, author, educator, and founder of the organization Prevention and Treatment of Traumatic Childbirth (PATTCh), 25-34 percent of women report traumatic births.

Not all those who experience a traumatic childbirth develop post-traumatic stress disorder (PTSD), but some do. Common symptoms of PTSD include, but are not limited to, anxiety, numbing, dissociation, insomnia, flashbacks, nightmares, hyperarousal, and impaired functioning. If not recognized and treated, these symptoms may persist and become chronic.

Traumatic birth experiences include premature births, still-births, unwanted interventions—such as unplanned or emergency C-sections—hemorrhage, difficult or long labors, perineal tearing, and separation from your baby. One experience may be traumatic for one person and not another. For example, those who have been sexually assaulted or abused may be more at risk for being retraumatized during labor and birth.

Postpartum PTSD often goes unacknowledged or isn't appropriately treated and can be confused with postpartum mood disorders. Postpartum PTSD can wreak havoc on a relationship. Sometimes the dad, or non-birthing partner, may have great difficulty understanding and knowing how to be helpful. Well-meaning spouses and professionals may encourage those who give birth to just put it behind them and move on, which can exacerbate the distress.

Finally, PTSD can interfere with a parent's ability to be present for their baby's needs and for their beloved. Left untreated, this not only causes ongoing struggle and suffering, but it also impacts attitudes toward, and experiences of, future pregnancies. Certainly, PTSD limits your ability to deal with conflict. Timely professional help is recommended.

Whether or not your symptoms meet the criteria for a PTSD diagnosis, if you struggle in the aftermath of a difficult birth, please explore ways to alleviate your suffering, such as mindfulness practices, somatic forms of release, journaling, and therapy. If you can do so without feeling triggered or retraumatized, telling your birth story to a safe person—a trusted, empathetic friend or family member—may help you process and diminish distress.

Breastfeeding Challenges

Breastfeeding provides many benefits to babies, such as an enhanced immune system and strengthened connections with nursing or chest-feeding parents.[8] Nursing is a physiological process tied to your baby's nutritional and attachment needs, and strong cultural messages exist about the importance, intuitiveness, and naturalness of breastfeeding. Because of the value attached to breastfeeding, when challenges occur, they not only can trigger infant distress, but they can also cause physical and emotional distress for the nursing parent, which can heighten relationship conflict.

Even when nursing is quite easy and positive from the start, the increased physical strain, sleep interruption, and on-call demands of the experience, including the tangible physical, visual, and emotional focus on the baby, can spark feelings of alienation and, sometimes, jealousy in spouses. This can, in turn, trigger conflict. Like breastfeeding challenges, these responses are normal occurrences in the transition to parenthood, and the entire family can benefit from an increased understanding and compassion from both breastfeeding and non-nursing parents alike.* If feelings of resentment or jealousy persist, a therapist or credentialed relationship coach can help you better comprehend and work through your emotions and prevent long-term impact on your relationship and family.

Special Needs Babies

Having a baby with special needs creates significant pressure and unique challenges for new parents. More extreme sleep

---

* See Tool 27, Honor Your Transition to Parenthood, for more guidance on navigating this transitional period.

deprivation, difficult medical decisions, additional and sometimes high medical costs, and feelings of grief and anxiety increase individual and relationship distress. Give yourself room to experience all your emotions. While the tools in this book will be helpful, you may need other resources to best address your baby's particular challenges and their impact on you and your relationship.

Childhood Trauma

Parenthood often stirs up unresolved childhood traumas that need attention, healing, and resolution. One perspective to hold is that becoming a parent provides opportunities—albeit sometimes demanding ones—to work through issues that would benefit from your care and attention anyway. Maybe you haven't been motivated to do the difficult work of healing trauma for yourself, but having a baby ups the ante: Now, you are willing to do it to be the best parent possible. Dan Siegel and Mary Hartzell's book, *Parenting from the Inside Out,* is a great resource on this subject.

Parenthood often stirs up unresolved childhood traumas that need attention, healing, and resolution.

You may also want to consider individual psychotherapy to help you separate your past issues from current reactions to parenting challenges.

Addiction

Addiction includes struggles with alcohol, drugs, sex, the internet, pornography, video games, food, gambling, exercise, and work. Basically, any substance use or activity that becomes compulsive and interferes with healthy life functioning is considered an addiction. If you or your mate struggle with addiction, Fight Right tools can help . . . to a point.

Depending on the nature and severity of the addiction, your capacity for healthy conflict resolution may be severely compromised unless you address it. If you struggle with addiction, you may need professional assistance, a treatment program, or a support group.

If your partner grapples with addiction, try to sort out what you cannot control from what you can. You cannot control or stop your spouse's addictive behavior. You can focus on healthy boundaries, self-care, and getting support for yourself. You can remain alert to the impact of your partner's addiction on your family, especially your baby, and speak to your spouse about your concerns. While you cannot force them to seek help, you can encourage them to do so.

Mental Health Challenges

If you have a significant mental health challenge, especially one that is untreated, professional assistance may be especially important when you become a parent. Challenges include significant struggles with depression, anxiety, OCD, borderline personality disorder (BPD), bipolar disorder, as well as attention-deficit/hyperactivity disorder (ADHD), and autism spectrum disorder (ASD). Coping with any of these conditions is likely more difficult during times of transition and stress, such as new parenthood. Getting professional help to better navigate those challenges takes the pressure off the relationship, supports the struggling parent, and enhances their ability to be as present as possible with their baby and the demands of new parenting.

Big-Picture Stressors

Becoming parents during a widespread health crisis or a natural disaster—such as an earthquake, hurricane, or wildfire—or in the midst of social or political unrest—increases individual and relationship stress, contributes to Fighting Wrong, and ramps up isolation, fear, and a more general loss of personal agency. The same holds true of persistent stressors that many parents face, such as poverty, racism, xenophobia, sexism, homophobia, transphobia, mentalism, ableism, and ageism, to name a few.

Perhaps because new parenting, too, sometimes feels out of control—moments when you fail to discern what your baby's cries communicate; times when no matter what you do, your baby refuses to fall asleep—big-picture stressors can exponentially increase your fight, flight, or freeze brain reactivity and limit or block your access to the mindset and tools to Fight Right.

Acknowledging those additional stressors and naming their negative impact on you and your capacity to connect with your spouse is sometimes all you can do in challenging times. Just as your ability to Fight Right ebbs and flows, so, too, does your competence to capably navigate those kinds of occurrences. Doing your best and refraining from judging what that looks like for you and your mate proves especially beneficial when an external stressor is at play.

Conclusion

What's next? How can you maintain what you have learned? How do new tools become habits? Practice, practice, practice.

There is no such thing as perfection with any of this. Yet using Fight Right tools will shift you away from the habitual go-to reactions that contribute to tension, misunderstanding, and relationship frustration. The only ways to create new patterns and habits are through intention, persistence, and repetition.

Will you sometimes take a step back after moving forward? Yes. That's a natural part of any learning process and of being human. Plus, you are more likely to regress when you're tired or stressed. Try to view those seeming setbacks as part of your growth, part of what it takes for you and your relationship to change in positive ways.

If your conflicts remain or become increasingly inflammatory, negative, or disruptive to your relationship and parenting satisfaction, or if you struggle to remember what first drew you to your spouse, we encourage you to quickly find a seasoned couples therapist or credentialed relationship coach to provide extra support and guidance.[9] Unfortunately, some people wait so long to seek help that they lose the capacity or desire to improve their relationships, a phenomenon especially tempting when faced with exhaustion and the financial and time constraints of parenthood.

Despite those obstacles, for the sake of your children's developmental health and your individual and relationship fulfillment, getting professional help tailored to your relationship's unique needs might be the best way to learn how to Fight Right, rekindle your connection, and save your relationship from separation or divorce.[10]

Whatever path you take, we hope you use this book as a resource to return to when the going gets tough. Revisit the tools and try to find ones that fit the areas where you need help at the moment. Follow the guidance and implement the tools to the best of your ability. There is no finish line, just an ongoing shared journey with your spouse.

> *Living with and learning from conflict is a core, lifelong part of human existence.*

At times, the relationship will go more smoothly with less conflict, and at other times, you will face significant challenges. Living with and learning from conflict is a core, lifelong part of human existence. When you hit your edge with each other again and don't know what to do, lean into it with curiosity and as much self-compassion and empathy for your beloved as you can muster. Good luck with your journey. Your commitment to Fight Right is an ongoing gift to yourself, your relationship, and your children.

Tools to Dig Deeper

We designed these tools to offer a deeper dive into some of the issues that contribute to Fighting Wrong and to assist you in your journey to Fight Right. They require more time and effort than the tools explored in previous chapters. If you delve into them, you will discover significant benefits to yourself and your relationship.

 ## TOOL 38. DIFFUSE PARENTAL SHAME

Parents are especially vulnerable to feelings of shame because the stakes of keeping babies physically and emotionally safe are so high. Many people experience a new level of fear and a heightened sense of responsibility in caring for a new little being. Plus, parents are particularly vulnerable to feeling judged and to judging themselves and their value as a person based on

> *Parents are particularly vulnerable to feeling judged and to judging themselves and their value as a person based on how well or how poorly they parent.*

how well or how poorly they parent. Not only does this leave little room for making the mistakes that accompany learning new skills in life, but it's also a recipe for shame.

No wonder a popular weapon in the Fight Wrong arsenal—and a common cause of disconnection—is shaming your spouse. Why? Because feeling ashamed is *so* uncomfortable that human beings tend to project it outward. Here, let's distinguish between guilt, which can be constructive, and shame, which tends to be debilitating. Whereas guilt arises from doing or saying—or not doing or saying—something you regret or consider a mistake, shame permeates your being. It takes shape in negative, critical "I am" and "you are" statements, beliefs, and accusations.[11]

Parenthood provides ample opportunities for both guilt and shame. For example, because you waited so long to change your baby's diaper, he got a rash. You regret your mistake and vow to react faster next time. That's guilt. Unfortunately, some of you might react to the same situation with internal shame and decide you are a bad parent because your actions hurt your child. With shame, there's no room to repair or change; your "badness" feels absolute and irredeemable.

Guilt and shame are vehicles for Fighting Wrong with your spouse when they make mistakes. To guilt them, you might say: "Why did you wait so long to change his diaper? Change it faster next time!" Shaming, by contrast, smacks of permanence: "What's wrong with you? You're a terrible parent!" While neither admonition is especially kind, the first scenario allows for corrective measures; the second precludes them.

According to shame researcher Dr. Brené Brown, parenthood and motherhood/fatherhood comprise two of twelve shame categories in North American society. Whereas the former relates to a range of parenting practices, e.g., "I'm a horrible parent because I yelled at my baby," motherhood/fatherhood shame is about how well or poorly you fulfill cultural expectations about being a mother or father. For example, some women experience shame because they work outside the home and aren't with their kids as much as they or the people around them believe mothers "should" be, while others feel ashamed that they cannot or choose not to become mothers at all. Both are forms of motherhood shame.

The remaining shame categories are appearance and body image, money and work, family, mental and physical health, sex, addiction, aging, religion, surviving trauma, and being stereotyped and labeled.[12] As this diverse list suggests, parenthood dovetails with or amplifies shame across multiple categories, which makes it an especially complex and vulnerable time of life.

The intersections between shame and new parenthood include:

+ Thinking there's something wrong with you because of how little you desire sex and intimacy in the days, weeks, or months after giving birth.
+ Feeling ashamed because of how much you want sex with your spouse even though you know she's exhausted.
+ Believing you're a failure because you struggle to make ends meet with the added costs of a newborn.
+ Thinking you're a horrible mother because you want to work outside the home.
+ Assuming you're a failure because you're a stay-at-home parent and don't earn money.
+ Deciding you're ugly because of how your post-birth body looks and feels.
+ Being certain you're a terrible parent because you feel impatient or irritable toward your baby.

+ Assuming you'll never be a good parent because of
  your own childhood trauma.

According to Brown, gender sometimes impacts shame. Whereas many women perceive shame as contradictory—e.g., you're too sexy *or* you're not sexy enough—Brown discovered that most men experience shame in a more singular fashion: You're a terrible breadwinner, an unskilled lover, or too soft, weak, or sensitive. Men's shame is often tied to failing to meet cultural, familial, or personal definitions of masculinity and linked to being perceived, or perceiving yourself, as weak.

Increasingly, though, men receive double-messages, especially when it comes to fatherhood: Be emotionally accessible to your spouse and baby and let your tender feelings show, *and* stay strong so your partner and kid can rely on you when the going gets tough; be home as much as possible *and* earn as much money as possible to provide for your family. Not only are these contrasting messages a bit crazymaking, but they also might trigger shame if you fall short in any of these areas.

Here are strategies to avoid or reduce the harm that shaming yourself or your spouse can cause:

+ When you use self-shaming language like "I'm a
  terrible parent," quickly reword your sentence and
  substitute "I did" or "I said" language. For example,
  "I made a mistake," or "I said something I regret."
  Practice similar revisions if you shame your spouse.

+ Test out Parts of Me Language (Tool 34) to better
  contain shame and counteract its absolute nature, e.g.,
  "Part of me feels like I'm a bad parent, while another
  part believes I'm a good parent who made a mistake
  with our baby."

+ If you notice yourself or your partner expressing contradictory or paradoxical expectations about your or their parenting:
  + Name the paradox, e.g., "I want to be with my baby as much as possible, *and* I also want to financially support my family as well as possible."
  + Let yourself or them off the hook by providing a timeline, e.g., "If I have to choose between being with my family and earning as much as possible, I choose [fill in the blank] because that's the priority in the next six to twelve months."
  + It also helps if you stop using harsh or extreme language. For example, instead of "You *should* be with our family as much as possible, *and* you *should* earn as much as possible," soften words and expectations: "I want you to be with our family as much as possible, and I want you to be a financial success. It might be hard to do both at once, and that's okay."

However you navigate shame, learning to differentiate it from guilt, and understanding that it commonly shows up for new (and seasoned) parents, alleviates its intensity and helps you better limit its impact on you, your relationship, and your family.

TOOL 39. GET TO KNOW YOUR SABOTEURS

You may possess firsthand experience with an Inner Critic: a judgmental voice in your head that speaks harshly to you when you make mistakes and calls you out when you fall short of expectations, whether your own or those of people whose opinions matter most. Your spouse, too, likely grapples with an Inner Critic. Because they feel like natural, unavoidable parts of you, Inner Critics often go unnoticed or at least unchallenged. Yet shifting how, when, and for how long your Inner Critic communicates with you and your partner offers benefits, including a decrease in Fighting Wrong. Fighting Wrong occurs when you face off against your spouse with the same kind of harsh judgment that happens in your inner world. Increasing your awareness of your Inner Critic's judgmental voice, then, not only creates a more harmonious internal environment but also supports your relationship because how you talk to yourself tends to be how you talk to others, including, and especially, your partner.

> *Fighting Wrong occurs when you face off against your spouse with the same kind of harsh judgment that happens in your inner world.*

Major life changes are prime triggers for a specific type of Inner Critic, what The Coaches Training Institute dubs a "Saboteur," a highly reactive part of you that shows up in auditory, behavioral, and emotional ways.[13] While the specifics of what activates Saboteurs vary from person to person, some aspects of new parenthood—learning a variety of baby-care skills; being responsible for a small human; and adjusting to shifts in your social life, intimacy, sleep patterns, and work-life balance—prompt many Saboteurs to try to take charge of you and your relationship. In these situations, your competent, adult, mature, grounded self—the discerning part of you that calmly evaluates decisions and changes from a place of thoughtfulness, empathy, and strategic planning—sometimes stays silent or emerges only intermittently.

Getting to know your Saboteurs—and helping each other recognize when they're activated—is another way to Fight Right and reframe at least some unproductive fights as part and parcel of learning how to adapt to the numerous changes you're facing together.

This list offers the most common auditory, behavioral, and emotional ways that Saboteurs manifest:

+ Insults, name-calling, other negative self-talk, or negative ways of speaking to others. This might be called "the language of shame."
+ The use of absolutes (always, never, impossible), either-or extremes ("I'm right and you're wrong," "You're either with me or against me!"), and rigid cause-effect thinking ("I won't survive another sleepless night!").
+ A critical, dismissive, sarcastic, agitated, or otherwise unpleasant tone of voice.
+ Commands and demands, such as: you or I should/ shouldn't, have to, better not.
+ Procrastination and other time-management issues.
+ Mild distraction, fogginess, lethargy, or a sudden onset of fatigue.
+ Mild anxiety.
+ Unhealthy habits.
+ Righteous, defensive anger.
+ Distancing, isolating, armoring, resistant, and numbing behaviors.[14]

Saboteurs likely developed during childhood as protective mechanisms in response to real or imagined threats. While your competent, mature self grows and evolves over time, Saboteurs usually remain underdeveloped and hypersensitive parts of you.

Although wishing them away seems like a great strategy, Saboteurs often dig in their heels when you feel most resistant to or just plain sick of them. Plus, as uncomfortable as they may be, Saboteurs have much to teach you about how you try to protect yourself and your relationship. Getting to know them brings your fears and what triggers those fears into your conscious awareness, where you can proactively reduce their negative impact.

How can you support your competent, mature, adult self—your "inner parent"—while reducing the impact of your reactive Saboteurs on you and your relationship? Familiarize yourself with the most common ways your Saboteurs show up. Notice what triggers them, explore what they hope to accomplish, and most importantly, resist the temptation to let them engage or argue with your spouse.

Here are strategies to help you do so:

1. When you notice any of your auditory, emotional, or behavioral Saboteurs, acknowledge that part (or parts) of you with a simple internal comment like "I hear you" or "I feel you."

2. If you and your spouse agree to be kind and gentle in your delivery, when one of you notices a Saboteur's speech patterns or behaviors, give each other permission to name it and request a break from the conversation.

3. When you recognize a Saboteur, get curious about its motivations, and ask yourself: "From what is it trying to protect me, the baby, or my relationship right now? What risks, downsides, or dangers would I face if I did or said the opposite of what it wants?"

4. Once you have a sense of some of your Saboteur's protections, inquire:
   a. How are my Saboteur's protective efforts helping my relationship or family right now?
   b. How do my Saboteur's efforts threaten or negatively impact the wellbeing of my relationship or family right now?

5. If your responses to 4.b are more numerous than 4.a, yet you still want some or all of the protections your Saboteurs are devoted to, consider sharing those protections with your spouse and, together, strategize more helpful ways to achieve them. For example, let's say that every time your partner enters the room when the baby is sleeping, your Saboteur prompts you to aggressively shush him. You quickly figure out that the Saboteur is trying to protect your baby from the distress of being woken up, and you from the further exhaustion and upset that come with the baby's sleep interruptions. To replace your reactive shushing, perhaps you and your spouse decide that if you put a Post-it outside the nursery door and then close it quietly, or you text him a snoring emoji during naptime, he'll understand that entering the room is a "no-no" and wait until the baby wakes up.

The specific strategies you devise are less important than shifting away from Fighting Wrong by inviting your competent self to take the lead and your Saboteurs to adopt a secondary role.

The more you and your spouse identify Saboteurs and limit the frequency with which they show up, the more capably you'll Fight Right and grow your ability to connect with your competent, mature, adult selves and each other.

 TOOL 40. LANDS WORK

This is an exercise created by the Center for Right Relationship that helps people better understand the way they differ from their partners by imagining they are independent nations with their own unique cultural practices; judicial systems; national cuisines; financial, banking, and trade policies; border patrol; immigration policies; parenting philosophies; religious and spiritual beliefs; and so on.[15] Lands Work is most helpful for issues of mild to moderate intensity. Even if you don't have time to explore all the steps, just adopting the perspective that you and your spouse are like countries unto yourselves allows for a more expansive and tolerant dialogue about your differences.

> **Adopting the perspective that you and your spouse are like countries unto yourselves allows for a more expansive and tolerant dialogue about your differences.**

Here's how it works: Choose a topic about which you and your beloved disagree. For purposes of illustration, let's pretend that you butt heads over what brand of formula to use to supplement breastmilk. We realize that some of you do not disagree about this topic, while others refuse to consider baby formula at all. Humor us and play along.

Find somewhere quiet—or as quiet as possible—to sit down and imagine that you're not an individual; you're an entire nation. We know it's an odd request! With that metaphor in mind, give your country a *neutral* or *positive* name that reflects your attitude toward the brand of formula you prefer, e.g., "Organic Land." Your spouse might name his land "Cost-Conscious Land."

Once you each come up with a name, consider the following questions and take notes to capture your responses:

+ What are your nation's guidelines regarding baby formula? Do organic ingredients override other considerations, or does pricing determine preferences?
+ What's most important to your country about its guidelines regarding baby formula? For example, is it that a baby's health is best supported by organic ingredients or that formula should be affordable and not put a strain on the budget?
+ When parents follow your nation's baby formula guidelines, what positive outcomes result for them and their families?
+ What fears arise in your country about the baby formula policies of other nations?
+ When citizens in your country have children with citizens of other countries, what helps them accept national differences and collaborate effectively, despite disagreements?

After considering these questions, invite your partner to play the role of an ideal tourist in your country[16]—someone genuinely curious *and* nonjudgmental—and ask them to join you on your side of the room. As a tour guide, introduce them to your nation's approach to baby formula (or whatever topic you actually choose) by explaining your policies on the topic, why they're important in your nation, and how they support babies and families. Please refrain from criticizing policies in other countries, especially your spouse's land.

After completing the tour, ask your mate to repeat back what they learned about your land. If they forgot an important detail or described something in ways that fail to capture your intent, gently revise or add to what they share.

Before touring your partner's country, try to clear your mind of preexisting judgments about their nation's policies to adopt an ideal tourist's perspective: curious and open to differences. Then, join your spouse on their side of the room. After your partner describes their nation's policies and priorities, feel free to ask any additional questions that occur to you. Before asking a question, take a moment to ensure it remains free of judgment or criticism.

Whether or not you agree with the stated benefits of their nation's policies, repeat your understanding of why the policies are important in their country and how they benefit citizens, especially babies and families. Remember, the goal is to *understand* why policies exist in their country, not agree with those policies.

Even if you disagree with most of their country's approach to the topic in question, come up with two or three things you align with, even if only partially, such as while you might not think organic ingredients override financial considerations, you agree that organic ingredients can be healthier than non-organic ones.

Once you complete both tours, head to a third location in the room to create "Our Land," the nation you occupy together. Feel free to come up with a more creative name than "Our Land."

Then, explore these ideas and questions together:

+ Name two or three ideas you find beneficial or agree with, even if only partially, from each other's national policies about the topic at hand. Add these to "Our Land's" policy.
+ Knowing each other's countries as you do now, and understanding each country's priorities, how can you jointly create an Our Land policy on the topic, with a view to honoring each nation's *highest* priorities, even if only partially?
+ Sustainable compromise depends on your ability to:
  + Accurately name each other's priorities.
  + Understand and describe *why* they are important to each of you.
  + Design joint policies that reflect mutual understanding. The outcome need not be fifty-fifty, especially if neither of you feels resentful and both of you feel heard and respected.

Whatever policies you craft for Our Land, write them down and keep them handy. In the future, if disagreements recur on this topic, consult the policies you created together for guidance. As time passes and your respective priorities change, revise your policies together. Feel free to revisit each other's countries at regular intervals to help maintain an open, curious, and nonjudgmental dialogue.

 ## TOOL 41. RELATIONSHIP VISION BOARD

Create a vision board to tap into the power of imagery and shared creativity. Plus, it can be fun! You can create a digital version using online images and arrange them in a printable document or poster. Or collect your favorite magazines—ones you're fine with cutting up—glue sticks and a large piece of foam board or cardboard.

1. Individually or together, thumb through the magazines and cut out images, words, or phrases that you find pleasing or catch your attention.
2. Lay them out on a large table and look at them together.
3. Ask your partner any or all of the following questions:
   a. What's your ideal vision for our relationship in the coming year?
   b. What's your ideal vision for our family in the coming year?
   c. How do we want to show up for each other?
   d. What's the best-case scenario for parenting together?
   e. What would constructive conflict look or feel like?
4. Using your responses as your guide, choose images, words, and phrases to position on your board.
5. Work collaboratively to experiment with placement and spacing.
6. Once you both like what you see, take a moment to ask:
   a. What, if anything, do we want to add?
   b. What would complete this Vision Board?
7. Find additional images, words, or phrases, if needed.
8. Glue all the images, words, or phrases in place.
9. Look at your completed board together and share any feelings or reactions.
10. Place your Vision Board where you will see it often, such as in your bedroom.

QUICK QUESTIONS

- What went well in creating your Relationship Vision Board?
- How can you apply what worked well to other aspects of your relationship?
- What might you gain by making this an annual activity?

TOOL 42. VALUES EXPLORATION

Understanding and exploring values helps couples feel more connected, avoid common conflicts, and navigate differences and disagreements with a neutral or positive versus critical or negative vocabulary. It's not necessary to share all the same values with your spouse, though it helps to know and accept how your values align and how they differ.

> *It's not necessary to share all the same values with your spouse, though it helps to know and accept how your values align and how they differ.*

Here are step-by-step instructions to create your values list(s). We define values as qualities, priorities, traits, standards, principles, philosophies, or life experiences that contribute to your sense of fulfillment and satisfaction individually, in your relationship, and as parents. Your unique combination of values is the "special sauce" that makes you, well, you! Often, you can discern your values in the traits you most appreciate and admire in others, including famous, historical, mythological, or even fictional figures.

Values can be more about aspiration than reality; your values don't always match how you live *right now,* yet they reflect who you aspire to be and how you most want to live. Behaving in ways that fail to align with your values often causes personal and relationship distress, so knowing your values increases your ability to recognize why you feel dissatisfied and how to feel better.

Disagreements with spouses—and pretty much everyone else—often emerge or worsen because of differences in one or more values, whether those are Individual Values (those you hold dear personally), Relationship Values (those important to your relationship satisfaction), or Parenting Values (those you hope to instill in and honor when raising your child). Knowing your values in each of these categories and discussing them with your partner increases your capacity for mutual understanding and teamwork, limits the scope of and fallout from conflict, and enhances Fighting Right.

While most people have more than a hundred Individual Values—yep, a hundred!—for the purposes of this exercise, select your Top Values in each of the three categories noted: the ten to fifteen *most important* to your fulfillment in the next six to twelve months.

Let's begin with your Top Individual Values (IVs):

+ Scan the *List of Possible Values* at the end of this chapter.
+ Write **IV** next to the fifteen or so values that are most important to your personal fulfillment *now* and for the next six months or so; these are your Top IVs.

+ String together those that seem interconnected, so they become a single value, e.g., honesty-authenticity-genuineness. Each string counts as one value. (Strings are optional, so no worries if values do not seem interconnected to you.)
+ Write a brief *definition* of each of your Top Individual Values. Not the dictionary definition, but your own take on what this value means to you.
+ Share your Top Individual Values list with your spouse.
+ When you read their list, consider exploring how, if at all, you can help them further honor their Top Values, and feel free to ask them to do the same with you.

Now, turn your attention to your Top Relationship Values (RVs):

+ Separately, create your lists of fifteen or so Top Relationship Values that you believe most support the wellbeing of your relationship together, *OR*
+ Create a Top Relationship Values List together, *OR*
+ Create a longer Top Relationship Values list that includes at least ten values you agree on, with up to six or so added ones that you individually, though not jointly, believe are crucial to relationship satisfaction.

Whichever option you choose, follow these steps:

+ Scan the *List of Possible Values* at the end of this exercise.
+ Jot **RV** for Relationship Values next to those that are most important to your relationship satisfaction *now* and in the next six months or so.
+ String interconnected values, if any, into a single value.

+ Together, or separately (depending on how you create your RV List), write a brief definition of each of your Top RVs.
+ Review your Top RVs List (or lists) and discuss which, if any, you've neglected recently. Feel free to ask each other questions, such as:
    + What's important to you about this Relationship Value?
    + How do you think this value enhances our relationship?
    + How can we better honor this value in our relationship now?

Finally, select your Top Parenting Values (PVs). You can generate this list separately or jointly, with a view to selecting values you most want to prioritize as you raise your kid(s).

+ Yet again, scan the *List of Possible Values*.
+ Write **PV** for Parenting Value next to the ones that are most important to your vision of your family for the first year of your baby's life.
+ String interconnected values, if any, into a single value.
+ Write a brief definition of each of your Top Parenting Values.
+ Get curious about the values proposed by your partner that differ from your most important PVs.
    + What's important to you about this Parenting Value?
    + How do you think it will enhance parenting?
    + How do you think it will benefit our child(ren)?
    + How do you think we can best honor this value?

Whew! You did it. You now have values to reference when you disagree with your spouse and when you want roadmaps to individual, relationship, and parenting fulfillment. Because values are dynamic and sometimes change over time, we encourage you to review them every year or two and update them as needed.

In addition to providing great insights into who you are and what you most want in life, values help you consider choices and make decisions. One reason big decisions often feel challenging or spark disagreements is that they often honor (or potentially honor) *and* overlook (or step on) values. Understanding which values are supported and which are sidestepped by the choices under consideration helps you clarify what's most important to you now and deepens your understanding of why you and your spouse sometimes disagree about the best option for yourself, your relationship, and your family.

Since many decisions involve compromise—including compromising one value in service of another—the more conscious and intentional you are about the values you are trying to honor and those you are willing to let slide, the more sustainable your decisions will be, both individually and with your beloved.

How else can you ensure your values remain helpful to you, your relationship, and your family?

- Familiarize yourself with the one or two values around which you feel the most "should" or "shouldn't" energy. Those are usually the ones Saboteurs—reactive, triggered parts of you—prioritize or deprioritize.[*]
- Post your values on the fridge so you can both reference them easily.

---

[*] See Tool 39, Get to Know Your Saboteurs, for insight into the reactive parts of you.

+ Import them into a note on your phone as an internal compass when you feel out of sorts, want to course-correct, or face an important decision.

List of Possible Values

This is a robust though not exhaustive list, so please add any entries that are important to *your* Values List.

VALUES LIST

Abundance	Acceptance	Accessibility
Accomplishment	Accountability	Accuracy
Achievement	Acknowledgment	Activeness
Adaptability	Adoration	Adroitness
Adventure	Affection	Affluence
Agility	Alertness	Altruism
Ambition	Amusement	Anticipation
Appreciation	Approachability	Articulateness
Assertiveness	Assurance	Attentiveness
Attractiveness	Audacity	Availability
Awareness	Awe	Balance
Beauty	Being the best	Belonging
Benevolence	Bliss	Boldness
Bravery	Brilliance	Buoyancy
Calmness	Camaraderie	Candor
Capability	Care	Carefulness
Celebrity	Certainty	Challenge
Charity	Charm	Chastity
Cheerfulness	Clarity	Cleanliness
Clear-mindedness	Cleverness	Closeness
Comfort	Commitment	Compassion

VALUES LIST

Completion	Composure	Concentration
Confidence	Conformity	Congruency
Connection	Consciousness	Consistency
Contentment	Continuity	Contribution
Control	Conviction	Conviviality
Coolness	Cooperation	Cordiality
Correctness	Courage	Courtesy
Craftiness	Creativity	Credibility
Cunning	Curiosity	Daring
Decisiveness	Decorum	Deference
Delight	Dependability	Depth
Desire	Determination	Devotion
Devoutness	Dexterity	Dignity
Diligence	Direction	Directness
Discipline	Discovery	Discretion
Diversity	Dominance	Dreaming
Drive	Duty	Dynamism
Eagerness	Economy	Ecstasy
Education	Effectiveness	Efficiency
Elation	Elegance	Empathy
Encouragement	Endurance	Energy
Enjoyment	Entertainment	Enthusiasm
Equality	Equanimity	Equity
Excellence	Excitement	Exhilaration
Expectancy	Expediency	Experience
Expertise	Exploration	Expressiveness
Extravagance	Extroversion	Exuberance
Fairness	Faith	Fame
Family	Fascination	Fashion

VALUES LIST

Fearlessness	Ferocity	Fidelity
Fierceness	Financial independence	Firmness
Fitness	Flexibility	Flow
Fluency	Focus	Fortitude
Frankness	Freedom	Friendliness
Frugality	Fun	Gallantry
Generosity	Gentility	Giving
Grace	Gratitude	Gregariousness
Growth	Guidance	Happiness
Harmony	Health	Heart
Helpfulness	Heroism	Holiness
Honesty	Honor	Hopefulness
Hospitality	Humility	Humor
Hygiene	Imagination	Impact
Impartiality	Independence	Industry
Ingenuity	Inquisitiveness	Insightfulness
Inspiration	Integrity	Intelligence
Intensity	Intimacy	Intrepidness
Introversion	Intuition	Intuitiveness
Inventiveness	Investing	Joy
Judiciousness	Justice	Keenness
Kindness	Knowledge	Leadership
Learning	Liberation	Liberty
Liveliness	Logic	Longevity
Love	Loyalty	Majesty
Making a difference	Mastery	Maturity
Meekness	Mellowness	Meticulousness
Mindfulness	Modesty	Motivation
Mysteriousness	Neatness	Nerve

VALUES LIST

Obedience	Open-mindedness	Openness
Optimism	Order	Organization
Originality	Outlandishness	Outrageousness
Passion	Peace	Perceptiveness
Perfection	Perkiness	Perseverance
Persistence	Persuasiveness	Philanthropy
Piety	Playfulness	Pleasantness
Pleasure	Poise	Polish
Popularity	Potency	Power
Practicality	Pragmatism	Precision
Preparedness	Presence	Privacy
Proactivity	Professionalism	Prosperity
Prudence	Punctuality	Purity
Realism	Reason	Reasonableness
Recognition	Recreation	Refinement
Reflection	Relaxation	Reliability
Religiousness	Resilience	Resolution
Resolve	Resourcefulness	Respect
Responsibility	Responsiveness	Respite
Rest	Restraint	Reverence
Richness	Rigor	Sacredness
Sacrifice	Sagacity	Saintliness
Sanguinity	Satisfaction	Security
Self-control	Selflessness	Self-reliance
Sensitivity	Sensuality	Serenity
Service	Sexuality	Sharing
Shrewdness	Significance	Silence
Silliness	Simplicity	Sincerity
Skillfulness	Solidarity	Solitude

VALUES LIST

Soundness	Speed	Spirit
Spirituality	Spontaneity	Spunk
Stability	Stealth	Stillness
Strength	Structure	Success
Support	Supremacy	Surprise
Sympathy	Synergy	Teamwork
Temperance	Thankfulness	Thoroughness
Thoughtfulness	Thrift	Tidiness
Timeliness	Traditionalism	Tranquility
Transcendence	Trust	Trustworthiness
Truth	Understanding	Unflappability
Uniqueness	Unity	Usefulness
Utility	Valor	Variety
Victory	Vigor	Virtue
Vision	Vitality	Vivacity
Warmth	Watchfulness	Wealth
Willfulness	Willingness	Winning
Wisdom	Wittiness	Wonder
Youthfulness	Zaniness	Zeal

References

American Psychological Association. (2018, October). Stress in America Generation Z. *American Psychological Association.* https://www.apa.org/news/press/releases /stress/2018/stress-gen-z.pdf

The Arbinger Institute. (2018). *Leadership and self-deception: Getting out of the box.* Oakland, CA: Berrett-Kochler Publishers.

Benson, K. (2017, October 4). The magic relationship ratio, according to science. The Gottman Institute. https://www .gottman.com/blog/the-magic-relationship-ratio-according -science/

Berens, R. (2012, December 10). The 10% rule: Parents, do less to connect more! *Huffington Post.* https://www.huffpost .com/entry/relationship-advice_b_2271797

Biehle, S.N. & Mickelson, K.D. (2012). First time parents' expectations about the division of childcare and play. *Journal of Family Psychology.* https://doi.org/10.1037/a0026608

Bridges, W. (2004). *Transitions.* Boston, MA: Da Capo Lifelong Books.

Brock, R.L. & Kochanska, G. (2016). Interparental conflict, children's security with parents, and long-term risk of internalizing problems: A longitudinal study from ages 2 to 10. *National Institutes of Health National Center for Biotechnology Information.* https://dx.doi.org/10.1017%2FS0954579415000279

Brown, B. (2008). *I thought it was just me (but it isn't): Making the journey from "what will people think?" to "I am enough."* New York, NY: Gotham Books.

Brown, B. (2010, June). *The power of vulnerability.* (Video). TED Talk. https://www.ted.com/talks/brene_brown_the _power_of_vulnerability

Brown, B. (2012, March). *Listening to shame.* (Video). TED Talk. https://www.ted.com/talks/brene_brown_listening _to_shame

Brown, B. (2012). *Daring greatly: How the courage to be vulnerable transforms the way we live, love, parent, and lead.* London, UK: Penguin Publishing Group.

Brown, B, (RSA). (2015, February 3). *Brené Brown on blame.* (Video). YouTube. https://www.youtube.com/watch?v =RZWf2_2L2v8

Caron, C. (2021, August 25). How same-sex parents share the mental load. *New York Times.* https://www.nytimes.com /2021/08/25/parenting/same-sex-relationships.html

Chamine, S. (2012). *Positive intelligence: Why only 20% of teams and individuals reach their true potential.* Austin, TX: Greenleaf Book Group Press.

Dimitroff, S.J., Kardan, O., Necka, E.A., Decety, J., Berman, M.G. & Norman, G.J. (2017). Physiological dynamics of stress. *Scientific Reports.* https://doi.org/10.1038/s41598 -017-05811-1

Eddy, B., Poll, V. & Whiting, J. & Clevesy, M. (2019). Forgotten fathers: Postpartum depression in men. *Journal of Family Issues.* https://doi.org/10.1177%2F0192513X19833111

El-Sheikh, M., Kouros, C.D., Erath, S., Cummings, E.M., Keller, P. & Staton, L. (2009). Marital conflict and children's externalizing behavior: Pathways involving interactions between parasympathetic and sympathetic nervous system activity. *National Institutes of Health National Center for Biotechnology Information.* https://www.ncbi.nlm.nih.gov /pmc/articles/PMC2918238/

Farr, R.H. & Patterson, C.J. (2013). Coparenting among lesbian, gay, and heterosexual couples: Associations with adopted children's outcomes. *Child Development.* https://doi .org/10.1111/cdev.12046

Finger, B., Eiden, R.D., Edwards, E.P., Leonard, K.E. & Kachadourian, L. (2010). Marital aggression and child peer competence: A comparison of three conceptual models. *National Institutes of Health National Center for Biotechnology Information.* https://dx.doi. org/10.1111%2Fj.1475-6811.2010.01284.x

Flanders, C.E., Gibson, M.F., & Goldberg, A.E. (2015). Postpartum depression among visible and invisible sexual minority women: A pilot study. *Archives of Women's Mental Health.* https://doi.org/10.1007/s00737-015-0566-4

Goldberg, A.E. (2013). "Doing" and "undoing" gender: The meaning and division of housework in same-sex couples. *Journal of Family Theory and Review.* https://doi.org/10.1111/jftr.12009

Goldberg, J. & Carlson, M. (2014). Parents' relationship quality and children's behavior in stable married and cohabitating families. *National Institutes of Health National Center for Biotechnology Information.* https://dx.doi.org/10.1111%2Fjomf.12120

Gottman PhD, J.M. & Gottman PhD, J.S. (2007). *And baby makes three: The six-step plan for preserving marital intimacy and rekindling romance after baby arrives.* New York, NY: Crown Publishing Group.

Gottman PhD, J.M. & Silver N. (2015). *The seven principles for making marriage work: A practical guide from the country's foremost relationship expert.* New York, NY: Harmony Books.

Graham, A.M., Fisher, P.A., & Pfeifer, J.H. (2013). What sleeping babies hear: An fMRI study of interparental conflict and infants' emotional processing. *Psychological Science.* https://doi.org/10.1177/0956797612458803

Harold, G.T., Aitken, J.J. & Shelton, K.H. (2007). Interparental conflict and children's academic attainment: A longitudinal analysis. *National Institutes of Health National Center for Biotechnology Information. https://doi.org/10.1111/j.1469-7610.2007.01793.x*

Hoppe MFT, K. & Tatkin PsyD, S. (2021). *Baby bomb: A relationship survival guide for new parents.* Oakland, CA: New Harbinger Press.

Insana PhD, S.P, Costello B.A., C.R. & Montgomery-Downs PhD, H.E. (2011). Perception of partner sleep and mood: Postpartum couples' relationship satisfaction. *Journal of Sex & Marital Therapy.* https://doi.org/10.1080/0092623X .2011.607053

Johnson, M. (2016, May 5). Have children? Here's how kids ruin your romantic relationship. *The Conversation.* https://theconversation.com/have-children-heres-how -kids-ruin-your-romantic-relationship-57944

Johnson EdD, S. (2008). *Hold me tight: Seven conversations for a lifetime of love.* New York, NY: Little Brown and Company.

Johnson EdD, S. (2013). Love sense: The revolutionary new science of romantic relationships. *Psychotherapy.net.* https://www.psychotherapy.net/article/couples/couples -therapy-sue-johnson-EFT

Katz-Wise, S.L., Priess, H.A. & Hyde, J.S. (2010). Gender-role attitudes and behavior across the transition to parenthood. *Developmental Psychology.* https://doi.org/10.1037/a0017820

Kessel, B. (2019, November 14). SOCAP19 – What is your financial archetype? https://abacuswealth.com/socap19 -what-is-your-financial-archetype/.

Lerner, H. (2017). *Why won't you apologize? Healing big betrayals and everyday hurts.* New York, NY: Simon & Schuster.

Maccio PhD, E.M. & Pangburn, J.A. (2011). The case for investigating postpartum depression in lesbians and bisexual women. *Women's Health Issues.* https://www.whijournal.com /article/S1049-3867(11)00030-2/pdf

Mammen, M.A., Busuito, A., Moore, G.A., Quigley K.M. & Doheny, K.K. (2017). Physiological functioning moderates infants' sensory sensitivity in higher conflict families. *National Institutes of Health National Center for Biotechnology Information.* https://doi.org/10.1002/dev.21528

Mannering, A.M., Harold, G.T., Leve, L.D., Shelton, K.H., Shaw, D.S., Conger, R.D., Neiderhiser, J.M., Scaramella, L.V. & Reiss, D. (2011). Longitudinal associations between marital instability and child sleep problems across infancy and toddlerhood in adoptive families. *National Institutes of Health National Center for Biotechnology Information.* https://dx.doi.org/10.1111%2Fj.1467-8624.2011.01594.x

MGH Center for Women's Mental Health. (2022, February 1). "Understanding the mental health impact of giving birth during a global pandemic." https://womensmentalhealth.org/posts/covid-19-childbirth/

Moore PhD, K.A., Kinghorn, A. & Bandy, T. (2011, April). Parental relationship quality and child outcomes across subgroups. *Child Trends.* https://www.childtrends.org/wp-content/uploads/2011/04/Child_Trends-2011_04_04_RB_MaritalHappiness.pdf

Palumbo, S., Mariotti, V., Iofrida, C., & Pellegrini, S. (2018). Genes and aggressive behavior: Epigenetic mechanisms underlying individual susceptibility to aversive environments. *Frontiers in Behavioral Neuroscience.* https://doi.org/10.3389/fnbeh.2018.00117

Pfeffer, C.A. (2010). Women's work? Women partners of transgender men doing housework and emotion work.

Journal of Marriage and Family. https://doi.org/10.1111
/j.1741-3737.2009.00690.x

Porter, C.L. & Dyer, W.J. (2017). Does marital conflict predict infants' physiological regulation? A short-term prospective study. *American Psychological Association.* https://doi.org
/10.1037/fam0000295

Reynolds, J., Houlston, C., Coleman, L., & Harold, G. (2014). *Parental conflict: Outcomes and interventions for children and families.* Bristol, UK: Policy Press.

Rhoades, G.K., Stanley, S.M., & Markman, H.J. (2009). The effect of the transition to parenthood on relationship quality: An eight-year prospective study. *National Institutes of Health National Center for Biotechnology Information.* https://dx.doi
.org/10.1037%2Fa0013969

Schwartz, R.C. (2021). *No bad parts: Healing trauma and restoring wholeness with the Internal Family Systems Model.* Boulder, CO: Sounds True.

Siegel, D.J. & Bryson. T. (2020). *The power of showing up: How parental presence shapes who our kids become and how their brains get wired.* New York, NY: Ballantine Books.

Siegel, D.J. & Hartzell, M. (2013). *Parenting from the inside out: How a deeper self-understanding can help you raise children who thrive.* London, UK: Penguin Publishing Group.

Simkin, P. (N/A). Birth trauma: Definition and statistics. *PATTCh.* http://pattch.org/resource-guide/traumatic-births
-and-ptsd-definition-and-statistics/

Tatkin, S. (2009, September 23). Welcome home exercise. YouTube. https://www.youtube.com/watch?v=V9FBdC2Kykg

Troxel, W.M., Robles, T.F., Hall, M., & Buysse, D.J. (2007). Marital quality and the marital bed: Examining the covariation between relationship quality and sleep. *Sleep Med.* https://dx.doi.org/10.1016%2Fj.smrv.2007.05.002

V., J. (2020, January 2). Fawning: The fourth trauma response we don't talk about. *The Mighty.* https://themighty.com/2020/01/fight-flight-freeze-fawn-trauma-responses/

Whitworth, L., Kimsey-House, K., Kimsey-House, H., & Sandahl, P. (2007). *Co-active coaching: Changing business, transforming lives.* Boston, MA: Davies-Black Publishing.

Wile, D.B. (2012, November 10). A one-page description of collaborative couple therapy. http://danwile.com/2012/11/a-one-page-description-of-collaborative-couple-therapy/

Wile, D.B. (2021). *Solving the moment: A collaborative couple therapy manual.* Las Vegas, NV: Self-pub.

Endnotes

1. In addition to the *highly* toxic conflict styles of verbal, emotional, or physical abuse—including bullying, gaslighting, and other coercive practices—some people possess a combination of traits that render them unable to Fight Right. Dr. Ramani Durvasula offers the acronym C.R.A.V.E.D. as a way to identify them: Conflictual, Rigid, Antagonistic, Victimized or Vindictive (or both), Entitled, and Dysregulated. If your spouse exhibits this combination of traits, please seek individual support from a therapist.

2. For an amusing explanation of blame, watch this RSA animated short by Dr. Brené Brown: https://www.youtube.com/watch?v=RZWf2_2L2v8

3. Permission to include the archetypes in *Fight Right for Your Baby* has been granted by Spencer Sherman and Brent Kessel.

4. While we often use the term "mom" to describe the person who gives birth, we understand that some who give birth identify as gender fluid, non-binary, or transgender and, therefore, are not represented by terms like "mother." To begin to remedy this linguistic bias, we often include gender-neutral language in this book.

5. Permission to include the first three questions in *Fight Right for Your Baby* has been granted by podcaster and meditation teacher Jonathan Foust.

6. Permission to include the Taking Time Tool in *Fight Right for Your Baby* has been granted by Mark A. Collin, creator of The Toolbox Project®.

7. For research on lesbians' and bisexual women's vulnerability to postpartum mood disorders, see Flanders (2015) and Maccio (2011). For recent research on fathers' postpartum mental health, see Eddy (2019). While we are unaware of research on postpartum mood disorders for trans parents or birthing parents who identify as gender fluid or non-binary, we suspect their risks are greater than for heterosexual cisgender moms, given the findings for lesbian and bisexual mothers, which underscore the added stressors of being a sexual minority.

8. Some trans and non-binary people prefer the term "chest-feeding," others favor "nursing," while some adhere to "breastfeeding" to describe feeding the milk produced by their bodies to their babies.

9. Well-trained, experienced, and credentialed relationship coaches can help with the vast majority of issues faced by expecting and new parents. There are, however, certain struggles usually best addressed with a licensed professional, like a psychologist, therapist, or social worker. The most common relationship struggles for which most coaches, credentialed or otherwise, do not receive extensive training include abuse, trauma, addictions, and mental illness. Some clients opt to work with both an individual therapist and a relationship coach, which can offer a helpful scope of support. Plus, some practitioners train as *both* therapists and coaches. Bottom line: Whoever you decide to work with, do your best to vet their credentials and experience to ensure they have the skill set needed to address your unique relationship struggles.

10. Whether or not your relationship endures, learning how to Fight Right with your coparent remains crucial to your baby's developmental health and wellbeing.

11. For more information on shame, watch Dr. Brown's two entertaining TED Talks: Brown (2010, June) and Brown (2012, March).

12. For more strategies to limit the fallout from shame and to learn about shame resilience, read Dr. Brown's books *Daring Greatly* and *I Thought It Was Just Me But It Isn't*.

13. We use the term "Saboteur" more expansively than The Coaches Training Institute, which limits it to a resistant, auditory inner critic triggered by change. Also, we use it differently than Shirzad Chamine who, in his book *Positive Intelligence*, offers a roster of ten Saboteurs. We appreciate Chamine's categorization of Saboteurs and his description of the contrasting inner Sage that offers an empowering, positive way to move beyond a Saboteur's hold. While Chamine suggests that you go to war with your Saboteurs, we encourage you to deepen your understanding of their protections and efforts to assist you, and then use tools to shift the balance of power from them to your competent, adult self. Our approach is aligned with Richard Schwartz's Internal Family Systems Therapy and his book of the same name.

14. Some of these issues—e.g., a sudden onset of lethargy, mild distraction, mild anxiety, numbing behaviors, and unhealthy habits—differ in important ways from chronic issues and clinical mental health challenges, such as sleep deprivation, ADHD, anxiety disorder, clinical depression, severe dissociation, addictions, and self-harm. Also, some of these concepts, like righteous anger, emerge for more reasons than the notion of the Saboteur captures, as they can be valid and empowering responses to discrimination and abuse.

15. Permission to include the Lands Work exercise in *Fight Right for Your Baby* has been granted by Marita Fridjhon of the Center for Right Relationship.

16. Another way of thinking about the ideal tourist is via what Shirzad Chamine calls the "Fascinated Anthropologist," which is "a keen observer and discoverer of what simply is, without trying to judge, change or control the situation."

INDEX

B

C

About the Authors

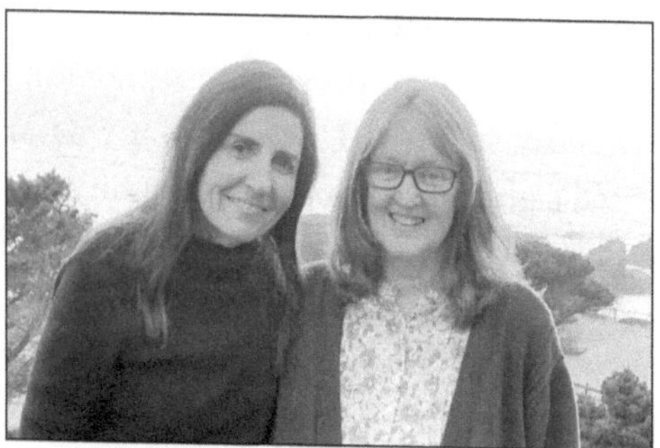

Rhona Berens and Tina Stanley

Rhona Berens is a Gottman Educator for *Bringing Baby Home*, a Gottman Leader for *The Seven Principles for Making Marriage Work*, a Certified *Positive Discipline* Parent Educator, and a credentialed coach who helps expecting couples and parents stay sane and stay together. As a mom to two fabulous, complex, and fiery children—not to mention an adorable dog and cat—Rhona knows firsthand that parenting takes its toll on even the best of relationships, which is why she tries and fails and tries again to walk her talk with her wife and kids. It's also why she offers expecting and new parents, and the perinatal professionals who support them, resources for connection and productive communication. Visit www.rhonaberens.com to learn more about Rhona's coaching services, workshops, speaking availability, and free resources.

Tina Stanley has been working as a psychotherapist, medical social worker, and hypnotherapist for over thirty years in private practice, and in medical and mental health settings specializing in perinatal mood disorders, parenting issues, and couples therapy. Currently, Tina specializes in working with clients to support their creative flow and spiritual healing. After repeatedly witnessing the "in the trenches" quality many couples experience as new parents, she has come to believe passionately in the value of proactive preparation and accessible, user-friendly support. Tina is also a wife and mother and has learned a great deal, especially humility and a sense of humor, from her own family life. Visit www.tinastanley.net to learn more about Tina's psychotherapy and hypnosis services.

You can also find Tina, Rhona, and their Fight Right insights on Instagram at FightRightBooks.

www.ingramcontent.com/pod-product-compliance
Lightning Source LLC
Chambersburg PA
CBHW061423160726

47995CB00003B/727